# COLUM'S OTHER ISLAND

### The Irish
### at Lindisfarne

# COLUM'S OTHER ISLAND

## The Irish
## at Lindisfarne

GARETH W. DUNLEAVY

*The University of Wisconsin Press*

*Madison,* 1960

*To my wife Elizabeth*

Published by the University of Wisconsin Press
430 Sterling Court, Madison 6, Wisconsin

Copyright © 1960 by the Regents of the University of Wisconsin

Printed in the United States of America
Composed by Superior Typesetting Co., St. Louis, Missouri, and
Printed by Cushing-Malloy, Inc., Ann Arbor, Michigan

Library of Congress Catalog Number 60–5657

# PREFACE

There is scant space allowed a researcher for acknowledging help received from many individuals and institutions. My great debt is to my teacher, the late John Webster Spargo, Professor of English at Northwestern University, from whom came aid always without stint. From Professor Frederic G. Cassidy of the Department of English, University of Wisconsin, has come constant encouragement along with helpful suggestions that have strengthened this study greatly. Professor Charles W. Dunn of New York University and Professor Elliott Van Kirk Dobbie of Columbia University have supplied valuable criticisms of the manuscript. For its deficiencies, the author alone is responsible.

I am grateful to the Research Committee of the Graduate School and the Regents of the University of Wisconsin for generous financial support given me in the summer of 1957.

My particular thanks go to Mr. Ben Bowman, Assistant Librarian of the Newberry Library and his staff, to staff members of the libraries of Northwestern University, Harvard University, and the University of Wisconsin.

I wish to thank the following for permission to make use of portions of the books indicated. Full bibliographical citations are given in the bibliography or the notes.

The Clarendon Press, for permission to quote from Gerard Murphy's *Early Irish Lyrics.*

Constable and Company, Ltd., for permission to quote from *Mediaeval Latin Lyrics* by Helen Waddell, and from *Selections from Ancient Irish Poetry* by Kuno Meyer.

Harvard University Press, for permission to quote from *Select Translations from Old English Poetry,* edited by Albert S. Cook and Chauncey B. Tinker, revised edition; and from *Baedae Opera historica,* translated by J. E. King, Loeb Classical Library edition.

The Henry Bradshaw Society, for permission to quote from *Félire Óengusso Céli Dé,* translated by Whitley Stokes.

Methuen and Co. Ltd., for permission to quote from R. A. S. Macalister, *The Archaeology of Ireland.*

Random House, Inc., for permission to quote from W. H. Auden's "Roman Wall Blues." Copyright by W. H. Auden, 1940.

The Standing Committee of the General Synod of the Church of Ireland, for permission to quote from Volume I of the *History of the Church of Ireland,* edited by Professor W. A. Phillips (1933).

For permission to reproduce in revised form parts of Chapters I and VII, which earlier appeared in *Mediaeval Studies* (1957) and *Philological Quarterly* (1956 and 1959), I wish to thank the editors of those journals.

I am grateful also to the following for permission to reproduce pages from manuscripts in their possession: Ambrosian Library, Milan; British Museum; Exeter Cathedral Library; Royal Irish Academy, Dublin; Schaffhausen Stadtbibliothek; Trinity College, Dublin.

To the Cartographic Laboratory, Department of Geography, University of Wisconsin, I would also like to express my gratitude for preparing the map for my book.

G. W. D.

*Milwaukee, Wisconsin*
*August 1, 1959*

# CONTENTS

# ILLUSTRATIONS

# COLUM'S OTHER ISLAND

*The Irish
at Lindisfarne*

Deer •

Iona (Hii)•

Coldingham
Lindisfarne
Melrose• •Farne Island
Bamburgh
Candida Bewcastle Cross
Casa + Ruthwell Cross
Bangor• Tynemouth Wearmouth
Nendrum •Moville Jarrow• •Hartlepool
Durham• •Whitby
Inisbofin •Mayo Gilling• Lastingham
Kells Ripon• Crayke
Clonmacnoise •Clonard York■
Clonfert •Durrow Barrow
•Kildare
Glendalough •Chester
Inis Cathaig Lichfield
Lismore• •
Ardmore• Cnobheresburg

•St. David's
Abingdon
Llancarvan• •Malmesbury
■Bath Canterbury
Glastonbury•
Exeter■ Winchester
•Dartmouth

0    75    150
Scale in Miles

• Monastery

■Other Places          + Stone Cross

Map showing monasteries and other points of cultural contact between
England and Ireland, A.D. 400–800.

Where is Duncan's body?
Carried to Colmekill,
The sacred storehouse of his predecessors
And guardian of their bones.
                    Macbeth II, 4

*Chapter*

# I

## ETHNE'S VISION
## AND THE FOUNDING
## OF IONA

Queen Elizabeth's Sheriff of Cork wrote excellent poetry and a history of Ireland a little less than objective despite its author's aim to "gather a likelyhode of truethe" and to "hunte out a probabilitye of thinges" about a people who lived in the seventeenth century much as their ancestors had in Cuchulain's day. Spenser's meritorious purpose is adopted for this account, and the reader is invited to re-examine truths and probabilities concerning the history of the Irish-created Northumbrian monastery of Lindisfarne from its founding in 635 to 793, the year of its devastation by Scandinavian raiders. Also offered is a synthesis of theories and discoveries relating to Lindisfarne's place as a channel for Irish influence exerted on the form of English scribal hands and books, on the form of certain stone crosses of northern England and Scotland, and on several Anglo-Saxon elegiac poems of the Exeter Book. Let us start with a brief description of the missionary activity in Scotland and Britain of Irish voyager-monks in the sixth century. Chief among these are St. Columba and his contemporaries, including SS. Brendan, Ciaran, Kevin, and Comgall. Their immediate achievements and their later reputations in Scotia Minor—the "lesser Ireland"—were to prepare

the way for Lindisfarne's establishment as one of the great spiritual strongholds of medieval Christendom.

*Sasanach* men of letters have never allowed the pre-Christian
heroes and heroines of Irish saga and romance to go unnoticed.
Cuchulain's flashing chariot wheels, beauteous Etain's sparkling
fountain, vanquished Anluan's severed head swaying at Conall's
waist have cast shadows that long have intrigued, enchanted,
perplexed, and charmed. From this literature of archaism came
a legacy exploited by Macpherson and ill-defined by Arnold.[1]

Only slightly less spectacular than the deeds of a shadowy
Irish Achilles were those of the early Irish wandering saints.
Around the names of Columba and Brendan there grew up a
body of literature including visions, navigations, and *vitae* that
rivaled that surrounding the name of the fifth century's St.
Patrick. In Tennyson's "Voyage of Maeldune" and Arnold's "St.
Brandan" the traveling churchmen are memorialized in English
literature. Neither were they neglected on the Continent. To the
ears of the poet of the *Inferno* and the *Purgatorio* may have
come the tenth-century *Vision of Adamnan,* the twelfth-century
*Purgatorium Patricii,* and the *Adventures of St. Columba's Clerics* composed in the twelfth century and found in the four-
teenth-century *Book of Lecan.*[2] In the wakes of the hide-and-
wicker curraghs were left tales of the sixth-century Irish
missionaries whose adventures on the "white-maned, white-
bosomed" sea rivaled those of the pre-Christian heroes.

Behind these self-exiled missionaries lay an Ireland spared con-
quest by Roman and Anglo-Saxon, an Ireland that had received
Christianity in the mid-fifth century from missionaries of Gaul
and western Britain and from refugee scholars of Gaulish schools
at Trèves, Marseilles, Bordeaux, and Poitiers. Both missionaries
and scholars brought conventional liturgical documents, a knowledge of pagan letters, and skills in literary letter writing and
oratory to take their place beside the written and oral traditions
of pre-Christian Ireland.[3]

Elusive and amorphous are the documents and names relating
to the fifth-century Christianization of Ireland.[4] For example,
Prosper of Aquitaine's *Epitoma Chronicon,* a contemporary work,

credits a certain Palladius with having been sent as the first missionary to Ireland from Rome in 431, but unlike his contemporary, Patrick, the man remains a phantom to this day.[5] There are also two shape-shifting, but forward-looking worthies—Camelac and Sechnall—who leave evidence of their Gaulish training in the form of Latin hymns and thus provide themselves with a precarious toehold on historicity.[6]

Slover undertook the important task of piecing together the story of Irish cultural relations with Britain before and during Patrick's time. He studied Gildas' account of Irish raids on Britain in the fourth century, the coin hoards in Ireland reflecting Irish looting in Britain, and St. Patrick's *Confessio* telling of that saint's youthful abduction from Britain by Irish slavers. From the tale of the *Expulsion of the Dessi* and the ogham inscriptions of Ireland and Britain came evidence of Irish settlement in Britain. Then there were those Irish royal exiles and fugitives described in the stirring *Destruction of Dind Rig* and the *Battle of Magh Rath* to show clearly that St. Columba was not the first Irishman to make the brief but rough passage to Britain.[7]

Sailing west to Ireland in the fifth century the curraghs had carried missionaries from a citadel of British Christianity, Candida Casa, now Whithorn in Wigtownshire, Scotland.[8] According to Bede ( *H. E.* III, 4 ), Candida Casa had been founded by Ninian, a Briton who had been given tutelage in Rome and had returned to his native land.[9] Irish tradition holds him to have been founder of two churches in County Tyrone and County Antrim.[10] Whereas the authenticity of Ninian's Irish enterprises is questionable, it is almost certain that missionaries left Candida Casa for northeastern Ireland and that their Irish converts returned there for training.[11]

From Menevia ( Ir. *Muine* ), the present port of St. David's near the extreme western point of the Welsh mainland, sailed other British missionaries. Menevia's founder was Dewi, or David ( fl. *circa* 500–600 ), to ecclesiastical biographers who set down his story about 1090.[12] David's death is recorded in the Irish *Annals of Tigernach* and a local St. David tradition existed in County Tallaght.[13]

A third embarkation point for British missionaries to the wild people of the *tuaths* was Welsh Llancarvan. Linked with Llancarvan in miscellaneous saints' lives are Finnian and Brendan.[14] Born at Myshall in County Carlow, Finnian (d. 549) became a monk in Wales. In the fifteenth-century *Book of Lismore* we read: "When the holy Findian grew up, he was taken to a bishop to Fortchenn, and read the Psalms and the ecclesiastical order with him. . . . Now when he reached the age of thirty he went over sea. He came to Tours. There he found before him an elder named Caeman. They were for a time together and they made a union. After that Findian went to Cell Muine [St. David's]. There he found before him three sages named David, and Gildas, and Cathmael."[15] Hagiographical tradition further ascribes to Finnian a period of thirty years' study in Britain after which he allegedly was diverted from a journey to Rome by an angel who, advising, "What would be given thee at Rome, will be given to thee here," ordered him back to Ireland to renew the faith of the people.[16] Obeying this holy mandate, Finnian established a vigorous monastic school at Clonard on the Boyne where he was to gain a reputation in hagiographical tradition as the great Magister of the "Twelve Apostles of Ireland," including Columba, Brendan, and Ciaran of Clonmacnoise. From the hand of Aileran (d. 665), a later student at Clonard, came a tract entitled *Interpretatio mystica progenitorum domini Jesu Christi*. An adaptation of St. Jerome's *De nominibus Hebraicus*, "it offers testimony to the early prevalence in the Irish schools of the allegorical method of Scriptural exposition."[17]

At least two other Latin *vitae* reflect the influence of Finnian's Clonard. In the first, the life of St. Molua (d. 622), we are told that Molua along with many others took instruction at the hands of Finnian, "virum sapientissimum," a title not lightly bestowed in the Middle Ages.[18] We read also of St. Ruadan of Lothra (d. 584), who left country and kin behind to join the *familia* ("monastic household") at Clonard as a student.[19]

Equally significant as the *vitae* for determining the sphere of influence of the traveling Irish churchmen are place-names and church dedications found in Britain.[20] Dedications to Finnian abound in Scotland. In the Cowal district of Argyllshire is the parish of Kilfinan.[21] Another dedication to Finnian is found in the name of the parish of Kilwinning in the Cunningham district of Ayrshire, southwest Scotland.[22] Five and one-half miles northwest of Port William in Mochrum parish, Wigtownshire, also in southwest Scotland, was a chapel dedicated to Finnian. Another dedication was the church of the parish of Bona, now included in Inverness-shire, northwest Scotland.[23] Finnian is remembered in central Scotland at Inverness in Glenlyon, Perthshire, where a chapel and well bear the name of St. Wynnin.[24] In northeast Scotland Finnian's name was given to chapels at Gartly parish, Aberdeenshire, and Abersnetwick in Monymusk parish. Two more Aberdeenshire parishes had St. Finnian as titular head of their churches.

Notable for his missionary activities in Britain and Scotland was St. Brendan ( d. 583) whom a ninth-century life of St. Malo identifies as a onetime abbot of Llancarvan.[25] Born on Fennit Peninsula, County Kerry, Brendan studied for five years under St. Ita, became Finnian's disciple, studied with Gildas at Llancarvan, and visited Columba at Iona. Between 558 and 564 he returned to Ireland to establish Clonfert in Galway, laying down an austere rule for its members. Surviving as an important center of learning, Clonfert was ransacked and plundered on five separate occasions after 895 by Scandinavian raiders.[26]

The *Breviary of Aberdeen,* a sixteenth-century Scottish collection of local traditions of saints' lives, echoes a chronicler's respect for Brendan's heroic vitality: "Brendan flourished among the Scots. When 532 years from the birth of Christ had passed: a man renowned for great abstinence and virtues, the father of nearly three thousand monks, he was held in the greatest esteem during those times for his extreme sanctity and doctrine."[27]

Known to the Middle Ages chiefly as the fabulous traveler to the "Isles of the Blessed," Brendan became one of the first heroes of voyage literature.[28] Translations into the vernacular of Latin accounts of Brendan's adventures met popular approval from late medieval mariners, map-makers, and explorers. The Brendan tradition is marked in northern France and the seaport cities of

northern Italy—Genoa and Venice. Popular in Germany and the
Lowlands, tales of Brendan's exploits were even translated into
Norwegian as late as the nineteenth century. By way of Ireland
and Wales, through traditions oral and written, Brendan became wrongly identified as a native of Britain.[29] An extract from
his Irish life in the *Book of Lismore* foreshadows the appeal of
his name to adventure-minded laymen: "Brenainn, son of Finn-
lug, sailed then over the wave-voice of the strong-maned sea, and
over the storm of the green-sided waves, and over the mouths of
the marvellous, awful, bitter ocean, where they saw the multi-
tude of the furious red-mouthed monsters, with abundance of the
great sea-whales."[30]

Dedications and place-names like those at Kilbrandane, Kil-
brennan, and Kilbramman, in Killarow parish, Islay, attest to
Brendan's popularity among the seafaring natives.[31] The Island-
men of Bute knew him as their patron and were proud to be
called "Brandanes." The rustic parishioners of Kilbirnie in Ayrshire, and those of Dunbarney parish in Perthshire, remembered
Brendan in their prayers.[32]

Scottish milkmaids still may croon a milking song that invokes
the Odysseus of the Irish *peregrini*:

> Come, Brendan from the ocean,
> Come, Ternan, most potent of men,
> Come, Michael valiant, down
> And propitiate to me the cow of my joy.[33]

The lonely herdsmen of the Western Highlands still may beseech
"the protection of Brendan of the ship" for themselves and their
charges.[34]

Ciaran of Clonmacnoise (d. 556) is the third sixth-century
Irish ecclesiastic with British contacts deserving examination
here. Born in Connacht, Ciaran learned that "after these things,
then, it was time . . . to go as a scholar to Findian of Clonard in
order to learn wisdom."[35] At Clonard, Ciaran was exposed to the
theological training for which Finnian's establishment was
noted.[36] Between 542 and 550 Ciaran founded Clonmacnoise in
West Meath at a key point on the Shannon near the Athlone
ford. Like Brendan, he laid down an extremely austere rule for

his monks. He died long before Clonmacnoise had earned its reputation for being second only to Armagh as a center of learning and literature.[37] According to *Chronicum Scotorum*, an abridged version of the eleventh-century *Annals of Tigernach*, Clonmacnoise survived seven burnings and plunderings between 816 and 1111. Undoubtedly Ciaran's ghost must have been shocked to see Ota, the mate of the Scandinavian chieftain, Turges, profaning the high altar of Clonmacnoise by giving prophecies from it.[38]

Ciaran ranged less widely than Brendan. In western Scotland there is one chapel dedication on Bute at Cilkeran in Rothesay parish; a second Kilcheran is on the island of Lismore; and in Kilcheroman parish, Islay, is found a Kilchieran. To the north is St. Queran's chapel at Strathmore in Halkirk parish, Caithness; in central Scotland lies Dail-ma-Chiaran ("the field of St. Ciaran") at Glenlyon in Perthshire.[39] Not long ago the efficacy of his name was still occasionally tested along with those of Patrick and Columba in a charm for afflictions of the eye:

> I place this charm to mine eye
> As the King of Life ordained,
> From the bosom of Peter and Paul,
> The third best amulet under the sun.
>
> Pour Mary, pour Bride,
> Pour Patrick, king of Laws,
> Pour Columba the kindly,
> Pour Ciaran, saint of power.[40]

Helping draw together Ireland and Scotland to a lesser degree than Ciaran was Comgall of Bangor (d. 601). Born in Ulster he studied under Finnian, and became founder of Bangor on the southern shore of Belfast Lough. Comgall's *vita* states: "Also in the seventh year after the monastery of Bangor had been founded, the holy father Comgall sailed to Britain, wishing to visit there certain saints, and to remain there for a time. And he founded a monastery there, in a certain village in the district of Heth; there he remained for a while."[41] Comgall's visit to Iona in company with Brendan is reported by Adamnan in his biography of St. Columba.[42]

One dedication to Comgall appears in eastern Scotland, at a church in Durris parish, Kincardine, formerly The Mearns,[43] but he is commemorated indirectly through his pupil, St. Mirren, a native of northern Ireland, who settled in Paisley about 560. There is a St. Mirren's Church in Sutherland, and another in the south at Kirkmirren in Kelton parish, Kirkcudbrightshire. The name of Comgall's pupil is given to the chapel at Inchmurrin in Loch Lomond, near where the Leven flows out of the loch.[44] No folk invocations and prayers to Comgall matching those to Brendan and Ciaran are to be found.

A probable veteran of many a voyage across the choppy Irish Sea was Kevin of Glendalough (d. 618), a Leinsterman educated by the Cornish missionary to Ireland, St. Petroc. Extant biographies reveal little of Kevin's British relationships. A life of Kevin, allegedly written by one of his pupils, gives Kevin credit for having rescued the former from danger in the "eastern land." Since the "eastern land" usually means Britain in Irish hagiography, the implication is that Kevin at one time visited Britain and brought back a pupil with him.[45] From Kevin's Irish *vita* comes the statement that kings of both Ireland and Britain chose to be buried in the cemetery at Glendalough, "for the love of God and Coemgen [Kevin]."[46] Many among them had apparently responded to a tradition that seven trips to lonely Glendalough in the Wicklow mountains equaled a pilgrimage to Rome.[47] Although commemorated by several church-dedications in western Scotland, Kevin is not invoked in the charms and incantations of that area.[48]

Hagiographical tradition ascribes British contacts to three other sixth-century Irish churchmen whose *vitae* can be sketched briefly before we turn to Columba of Iona. The first of this minor group is Senan (d. 560), who founded a monastery at Inis Cathaig (Scattery Island in the Shannon Estuary), visited Rome, and returned to spend time with St. David in Wales. Senan founded several more churches and monasteries in Ireland, finally settling at his own Inis Cathaig, where he died and was buried.

Another member of the second order of Irish churchmen having British contacts is Cainnech of Aghaboe (d. 600), who is mentioned several times in Adamnan's *Vita S. Columbae* and is reputed to have studied with Finnian of Clonard at Llancarvan in Wales. After spending much of his early life in the Western Islands, he voyaged back to Ireland, to found a monastery at Aghaboe.

Finnian of Moville (d. *circa* 575) is reputed to have become a monk in Scotland, and to have been ordained in Rome. He is said to have brought back Biblical manuscripts, possibly introducing St. Jerome's Vulgate to Ireland. Finnian later became the founder and first abbot of the monastery at Moville. Moville's reputation as a center of learning is indicated by the record of accomplishment of its most famous alumnus, Marianus Scotus (d. 1088), known as a skillful transcriber of manuscripts and as the founder of the monastery of St. Peter's at Ratisbon.

The Irish ecclesiastic about whom history can have no doubt and whose skill and energy as a missionary gave the impetus for Christianity's arrival in Northumbria in 635 is Columba of Iona, greatest of Finnian's disciples. Here is no half-wraith, but a flesh-and-blood figure born in 521, sixteen years before the reported death of King Arthur, and dying in 597, the year Augustine landed in Kent. His name, that of his monastery at Iona lying off the west coast of Argyllshire in the Hebrides, and the name of his most celebrated successor—Bishop Adamnan (d. 704)—will appear often in following chapters.

"Noble in sooth was Colum Cille's kindred as regards the world," proclaims the entry in the *Book of Lismore* compiled in the latter half of the fifteenth century.[49] " . . . of the kindred of Conall, son of Niall was he," continues this Irish life.[50] We are told that this Irishman of royal blood, in line for the chieftain's portion, turned his back on his inheritance of power and "put it from him for sake of God."[51] His mother, Ethne, awaiting his birth had seen a vision. Ethne, "daughter of Dimma mac Noe, son of Eochaid, son of Cairbre the poet, son of Ailill the Great, son of Breccan, son of Fiacc, son of Daire Barrach, son of Cathair the Great"[52] had watched "a great mantle . . . stretched from Insi-mod [islands off the coast of Mayo] to Caer-Abrocc [York] and every colour was present in it."[53] More than a millennium later came verification that the aurora borealis probably was wit-

nessed in 521 and 522 in both Ireland and Britain along the typi-
cal auroral arc extending WNW-ESE. To medieval men and
women, northern lights often heralded the birth of a great figure. His biographer, Adamnan, tells that the flashing streamers
of light marked Columba's birth and death.[54]

To the compiler of one martyrology he was "Colum fair,
mighty form, face ruddy, broad, radiant,/ body white, fame without falsehood, hair curly, eye gray, luminous."[55] His voice could
be heard at fifteen hundred paces, a fact recalled vividly by
witnesses at Iona who watched him chase a thief's boat into icy
water up to his knees, bellowing curses.[56] This voice had been
raised in battles and brawls long before he left Ireland for Iona.
Directly or indirectly he was involved in no fewer than three
such matches, the earliest occurring the year before his sailing
for Britain.[57] From oral and written sources his biographer was
to reconstruct the day-to-day routine of the monastery at Iona
presided over by this amazing man. With a channel on its east
side sheltered from the winds, with its green turf for pasturage
and its eastern slopes for grain, with flounders and seals swarm-
ing in the Sound of Iona to supply food and oil for illumination,
Iona was as self-contained as Finnian's Clonard or Brendan's
Clonfert.[58] But its leader was frequently restless. A trip to Ireland came in 585 with visits to Durrow, which he had founded
years earlier, and to Clonmacnoise on the Shannon. Thanks to
Adamnan's *Vita S. Columbae*, we can follow the saint's comings
and goings and his daily tasks at Iona, and can see him as he
examines the handiwork of the scribes in the scriptorium, plays
host to a pagan prince who has come to Iona for baptism before
death, and greets fellow monks who have guided their curraghs
through the stormy sea in search of solitude. When he uttered
his last prayer in Iona's chapel he could look back on active days
of organizing new churches among Christians in Dal Riata (Scotland) as well as in Ireland.[59] No less than thirty-seven churches
in Ireland were either founded by or dedicated to Columba. In
Scotland among the fifty-three dedications to Columba are
churches and chapels at Tannadice, Banffshire, Fordyce, Inver-
nesshire and Perthshire.[60]

Like his lesser contemporaries, he is amply represented in the humble literature of incantations and invocations. As late as 1860 an annual sacrifice to the sea on St. Columba's Day in return for a heavy sea-weed harvest was offered by maritime Scots. In company with that of Brendan his name is found in a milking song. It is invoked in herd blessings, charms for diseases of the eye and indigestion, a charm for the churning of butter, and a prayer against slander.[61] His name could do yeoman service also in charms for toothache and breaks and sprains.[62] The Scottish-Gaelic peasants had chosen well among the ecclesiastical heroes. On one occasion, Columba's sign of the cross had held off a ferocious monster threatening to devour a certain Lugne Mocumin as he swam across a stream to recover an object on the opposite bank for the saint. Why should not the name of such a man prevail against lesser devils whose pranks might spoil the butter and cause the jaw to swell?

Columba did his work well. Bede would write of "Hy: the monastery of which island was no small time the head house of all the monasteries almost of the northern Scots and of all the Redshanks, and had the sovereignty in ruling of all their people" (*H. E.* III, 3).[63] The *vallum* ("rampart") surrounding the original establishment is still visible, but except for the chapel, the architectural remains belong to the eleventh century or later.[64] An Anglo-Saxon coin-hoard discovered there recently testifies to Iona's drawing power as late as the tenth century. Nearly 350 silver coins ranging in date from 925 to before 991 may be spoils brought back by Viking raiders active in England in the tenth century.[65] Possibly Irish raiders paused there on the return trip from Britain to leave a thank offering for successful plundering. Perhaps the coins were intended to honor the memory of a king interred there.

Knowledge of the former custom of the burial of Irish, Scottish, and Norwegian kings at Iona survived to Dr. Johnson's time. Though appalled at the grossness of the islanders, the lack of either church or school, the cow dung on the floor of the nunnery chapel, Johnson could not go "unmoved over any ground which has been dignified by wisdom, bravery, or virtue" whether Marathon or Iona.[66] Boswell's piety was stirred to the extent that he knelt alone in prayer at the foot of St. Martin's Cross and lingered in the ruined cathedral to address "a few words to St. Columbus."[67] Wordsworth, also, paid his respects to Columba upon surveying the ruins of Iona and recollecting its past with "a thoughtful sigh."[68]

But long before these pilgrimages to Iona by *Sasanach* poets, the names of Finnian, Brendan, and Columba lived on in numerous church dedications in Scotland and the Hebrides made by their converts, by missionaries working out of Iona, and by Irish settlers. Saintly names given to churches, chapels, and wells and family names derived from names of saints[69] corroborate the accounts in Irish hagiography of the saints' visits to Britain and reflect hard-earned and sustained respect paid churchmen whose theology had come originally from St. David's, Candida Casa, and Llancarvan. Invocations to "Brendan of the Ship" and "Brendan from the Ocean" came from those who best appreciated the seamanship of an ecclesiastical sea hero. Like Brendan, Columba of Iona had earned the folk's highest accolade in the form of dedications, prayers, and charms. Both Brendan and Columba had performed daring acts in the face of formidable forces of nature—quickly roiled seas, savagely relentless rains, and forbidding, lowering mountains. To the people of *Scotia Minor* and to the Northumbrian converts of 635 and later, it seemed a further miracle that the successors of these sixth-century ecclesiastical demigods should make their way across the Irish sea in the pitching curraghs.[70] Through passes and gaps overlooked by ancient grim hill forts, down ridgeways and Roman roads, they came to Northumbria to signal with their arrival a new phase in a tradition of cultural contact unbroken since the Bronze Age between Ireland and the region called aptly Britain's "Highland Zone."[71]

Despite increasing hostility directed against it by the Anglo-Romans, Irish monastic culture at Lindisfarne was to leave a lasting imprint on the manuscripts, stone crosses, and literature of Northumbria. Fashioners of that imprint were the "sons" of Columba whose relationships with Northumbrian strong men of the seventh century are next to be considered.

But fain Saint Hilda's nuns would learn
If on a rock, by Lindisfarne,
Saint Cuthbert sits and toils to frame
The sea-born beads that bear his name.
                                    Marmion II, 16


*Chapter*
# I I

## SAINTS AND STRONG MEN
## AT LINDISFARNE AND BAMBURGH

The American consul at Liverpool, aboard the train running
from Berwick to Newcastle on the afternoon of May 7, 1856,
caught only a fleeting glimpse of a ruined abbey rising from a
low-lying island separated from the mainland by three miles of
oozing sand flats. Had Nathaniel Hawthorne been privileged to
view Lindisfarne from aloft, remembering his guidebook he
would have been struck by the grim irony in the fact that the
island's thousand acres of sand and basalt lie in the shape of an
ax.[1] The handle tapers northeast toward Berwick and the mouth
of the Tweed; the head of the ax faces south toward Bamburgh
Castle squatting atop a rocky mainland promontory across seven
miles of churning North Sea.

About the bloody incidents in Bamburgh's history after Lindisfarne's founding we might well echo Milton's "such bickerings to
recount . . . what more worth is it then to chronicle the Wars
of Kites, or Crows." At this seat of Northumbrian political power
and intrigue knives flashed as enemies without and conspirators
within its walls murdered or deposed thirteen of fourteen kings
in one century.[2] Occasionally neighboring Lindisfarne was
brushed by this hate and violence. Once a traitorous prince
sought sanctuary at its altar, to be snatched away by the retain-

ers of an outraged king; an uneasy king abandoned his *gifstol* to join the *familia;* and a slain king's head was buried in its church-yard. Such dramatic events tend to obscure the fact that the relationship between bishops and kings after 635 was mainly a fruitful one, furthering the development of Lindisfarne as a dissemination point for Irish monastic culture. It is a brief account of this relationship and its role in Lindisfarne's growth and expansion up to the time of the shattering Scandinavian attack of 793 that is offered in this chapter.

In 635, less than half a century after Columba's death, a member of the Iona *familia* named Aidan, after sailing the Firth of Lorne and the Sound of Jura, proceeded on foot over intervening headlands to the Firth of Clyde. Once across, he followed the Roman military road lying behind the Antonine Wall to its eastern terminus on the Firth of Forth. Traveling southeast he passed near present Edinburgh, following ridgeways and trails leading to Bamburgh.[3] Along this same route some time after 617 had traveled the boy princes Oswald and Oswy, first fleeing Northumbria to seek refuge at Iona, then returning to assume rightful power.

Of Aidan little is known before he led the mission to Northumbria. He is described by Bede as a meek, godly, and sober member of the Iona community during Seghine's abbacy (623–652). He may have served as an early bishop of Inis Cathaig (Scattery Island in County Clare), going to Iona to undertake missionary work before his departure for Bamburgh.[4] Undoubtedly his way at Bamburgh was smoothed because of the years spent by King Oswald in exile at Iona. The bell forged in the brazier's shop had summoned the boy prince and his retinue to Columba's church for their baptism. He had strolled the square separating the stone beehive cells used as living quarters from the rectangular wood-and-wattle structures constituting church and school.[5] Fact and legend about Iona's founder, later passed on to Adamnan for his *Vita Columbae,* had been related to the young Oswald. He had stood before stone crosses erected in Columba's memory and studied the stoneworker's handiwork. Years later, on the eve of the battle of Heavenfield, he was to

raise a wooden cross before his retainers with his own hands—
witness to his faith in God *and* Columba to bring victory.[6] Oswald had shared also in the intellectual life at Iona. His fingers
had formed the round letters of the semi-uncial Irish script, first
on wax tablets and then on vellum scraps from the scriptorium.
He had touched manuscript fragments of Horace and Virgil
reposing in book-satchels along with the writings of St. Augustine
of Hippo and newly-copied missals, Psalters, and prayer-books.

The influence of his Iona stay on Oswald was a lasting one.
His piety was to leave its stamp on his eight-year reign. His
thanes would come to accept their king's habit of praying from
Matins to sunrise; they were to listen to him in his role as the
untiring interpreter of Aidan's Irish sermons. At thirty-eight Oswald, like his predecessor Edwin, was to fall beneath the sword
of the relentless Penda of Mercia. At Penda's command the severed head and arms of Oswald were nailed to poles and hoisted
aloft to remain until Oswy retrieved them a year later. The head
Oswy ordered buried in the churchyard at Lindisfarne; the arms
and hands were enshrined at Bamburgh.

But Aidan's involvement in this tragedy lay ahead of him, the
second member of the Iona *familia* to answer Oswald's request
for a churchman to reconvert his people after their apostasy
following the death of Edwin in 633. The first cleric dispatched
from Iona had returned claiming that the Northumbrians could
not be tamed. Now before Oswald stood this strange figure with
head shaved ear-to-ear in the Irish style, looking much as Columba had when he presented himself to the Pictish king nearly
a century earlier.

In short order, carts hauling beams, wattle, and thatch moved
over the sand flats toward the island site granted Aidan by
Oswald. Future donations from friendly Bamburgh rulers were
to increase the monastery's holdings until by the time of Bishop
Cuthbert's reign (685–88), according to the account given in the
tenth-century *Historia de Sancto Cuthberto,* the land of Lindisfarne incorporated an area wider than Islandshire and Norham-
shire, its limits in the twelfth century.[7] In 674 came additional
land for establishing anchorite cells and hospices for pilgrims:

"Post hoc bellum [battle for the possession of Lindsey] dedit
Egfridus rex sancto Cuthberto Carrum [Carham], et quicquid
ad eam pertinet."[8] In 737 Lindisfarne benefited from the gener-
osity of King Ceolwulf, who found it prudent to exchange crown
for tonsure in that year: ". . . he granted an exemption and
immunity to all the churches and religious houses within his
realm, from all public taxes, works, and burthens, except only
(as was always usual) the building of castles and bridges. He
brought great revenues to the church, and granted in perpetuity
a large territory of land. . . . "[9]

The warm accord between King Oswald and Aidan is attested
to by Bede (*H. E.* III, 6). Aidan blessed Oswald's arm after the
sovereign performed an auspicious deed of charity and the arm
remained incorruptible, presumably even after being chopped
off at Penda's command to wither and bleach in the sun (*H. E.*
III, 6).[10] Aidan accepted large gifts of money and jewels from
various royal retainers to purchase the release of slaves and
"many of such . . . he made after his scholars, and by bringing
them up in learning and virtue advanced them to the degree of
priesthood" (*H. E.,* III, 5).[11] Long after Oswald's head had
been buried at Lindisfarne Aidan remained loyal to the strong
men at Bamburgh. In 651 Penda, the indomitable pagan rival
of the Northumbrian Christian kings, laid siege to Bamburgh
"pulling in pieces the hamlets which he found in the neighbour-
hood of the city, [and] carried thither a very great quantity of
beams, rafters, partitions, wattles and thatch . . . " (*H. E.* III,
16).[12] Piling this material against the walls, he ignited it, determined to burn out his enemies. From a vantage point on Farne
Island Aidan prayed for heavenly intervention and the wind
shifted to blow the searing flames into the faces of the assaulters.

Under Aidan's guidance, after 635 there developed a friendly
relationship between the Irish monks and the brethren on the
mainland. Bede reports that "upon the Sundays ordinarily the
people flocked eagerly either to the church or to the monasteries,
not for belly cheer but to hear the word of God, and if any of
the priests came by chance abroad into the village, the inhabi-
tants thereof would by and by gather together about him. . . .

For neither had either the priests themselves or the clergy other reason to come into the villages but only to preach, to baptize, [and] to visit the sick" (*H. E.* III, 26).[13]

Aidan was first of all a teacher, and his influence on his English students was quickly appreciated by Bede whose own life had been given over to learning, teaching, and writing. Of one of Aidan's most successful pupils Bede writes: "Chad then being consecrated bishop began shortly to be zealous in care for ecclesiastical truth and purity of doctrine; to apply his heart to lowliness, abstinency and study; to visit continually the towns, country places, cottages, villages, houses for the sake of preaching the Gospel, not making his journey on horseback but going on foot as the apostles used. For he was one of Aidan's scholars and laboured to instruct his hearers in the same way of life and behaviour after the example of Aidan and his own brother Cedd" (*H. E.* III, 28).[14]

Aidan's success as a converter of heathen rivaled that of Columba, according to the sixteenth-century historian, Hector Boece:

> This Adanus he baptist in sevin dais,
> Of men and wemen into taill wntald,
> Then fyftene thousand baith of ʒoung and ald;
> With greit blythnes, baith of ald and ʒing,
> And speciallie of gude Oswald the king,
> This Adanus that tyme without ganestand,
> Wes maid bischop of all Northumberland.
> Richt mony men than of religioun
> And secular men of greit deuotioun,
> To Adanus out of Scotland tha ʒeid,
> Him to supple in his mister and neid,
> The faith of Christ amang thame for to plant,
> For in that land the kirkmen were richt skant.[15]

Even Gaimar, the twelfth-century Anglo-Norman chronicler who wrote of Christianity's success in Northumbria giving little heed to Lindisfarne and its Irish affiliation, had to acknowledge the fame of Bishop Aidan and King Oswald.[16]

Oswald, "always humble, gracious, and liberal to pilgrims and the poor,"[17] was outlived by Aidan, but the tradition of amity

between these two men helped set the pattern for monastic organization noted by the chroniclers of Durham and Northumbria
as late as the eleventh century.[18] By the year of his death in
651, Aidan directly or indirectly had been responsible for founding Irish-manned monasteries at Lastingham, Tynemouth, Whitby, Barrow, Coldingham, and Hartlepool, as well as a fair number
of churches whose records have vanished.

Aidan's successors maintained the spiritual and intellectual discipline of Lindisfarne after the pattern set at Iona. Finan, in his
tenure (652–61), sent forth to Mercia missionary parties composed of Irish monks and Northumbrian converts, while behind
them the *familia* rebuilt the church, using sawed oaken timbers
and reed thatch, *more Scottorum* (*H. E.* III, 25). In the person
of Colman, who ruled from 661 to 664, Irish influence remained
unbroken at Lindisfarne. Trained at Iona, he witnessed the con-
troversies over Easter and the tonsure settled in favor of Rome
at the Council of Whitby (664). After King Oswy's decision in
favor of Rome, Colman assembled a group of Irish and Northumbrians and, leading them to Ireland by way of Iona, re-
established at Mayo the monastic routine they had maintained
at Lindisfarne.[19] Colman was succeeded at Lindisfarne by Tuda
(664), "who had been instructed and ordained bishop among
the South Scots [Irish] . . . " (*H. E.* III, 26).[20] A plague
snatched away many members of the community, including
Tuda himself, in 664.[21] But despite this calamity which created
despondency and caused suicides outside the *vallum*, Northumbrian converts continued to flock to Irish monasteries for instruction.[22] It is significant that the attraction of Irish learning
remained strong in the year following the decision at Whitby
and that the fame of Clonard, Clonfert, and Columba's Durrow
was undiminished.

King Oswy apparently had intended to appoint Wilfrid of
York to the bishopric of Lindisfarne, but after his personal tri-
umph over the Irish at Whitby, Wilfrid had departed for France
where he was to remain for two years.[23] Meanwhile, under Eata's
rule Irish monastic discipline continued to be exercised at Lindisfarne, for he was "one of the twelve scholars of Aidan, which
at his first coming as bishop he took out of the English nation

to be brought up in Christ . . . " (*H. E.* III, 26).[24] In 685 occurred the unwilling acceptance of the episcopate by Cuthbert
who, though not Aidan's student, had received Irish training at
Melrose and was himself possibly of Irish lineage.[25] During his
three-year rule at Lindisfarne, Cuthbert acquired a reputation
for great saintliness that assured him careful notice by chroniclers as late as the eleventh century.[26] Summoned to rule Lindisfarne from his hermit's cell on Farne Island, Cuthbert could
think back to the time when he used to leave Melrose for two
or three weeks, walking through the remote hills to seek out
converts where, according to Bede (*H. E.* IV, 27), other missionaries and teachers dreaded to visit.

At Cuthbert's death, March 20, 687, his body became a symbol
to succeeding generations of Northumbrian Christians of the
piety, humility, and dedication of the Irish-trained monk. Robed
in vestments and wrappings, he remained buried beneath the
stone floor on the south side of the altar of the church at Lindisfarne until 698. In that year the allegedly uncorrupted remains
were exposed to satisfy the curiosity of the brethren and to stim-
ulate pilgrimages. The body was then laid in a new and elaborately carved wooden coffin, fragments of which are still preserved at Durham Cathedral. With Lindisfarne under threat of
Norse attack in 875 it was understandable why the *familia* sought
sanctuary in Ireland for its saintly relics. Cuthbert's coffin was
opened hastily and in it were placed the supposed head of King
Oswald and Aidan's bones. Select members of the *familia* carried
this holy burden to the mouth of the Derwent in Cumberland,
near the present town of Workington. Ill omens, including high
tides, decided the band against carrying out the planned journey
to Ireland and they returned to Crayke in Yorkshire with their
burden. The coffin was taken from Crayke to Chester-le-Street
where it attracted gifts of land, money, and jewels from Northumbrian kings until the invasion of 995, when it was removed to
Ripon for safekeeping. Remaining there from spring to autumn
of that year, it was carried to Durham, where it lay until 1069–
70, when it was moved temporarily to Lindisfarne at the ap-
proach of William the Conqueror from the south.[27]

During the episcopates of Eadbert (688–98) and Eadfrith

(698–721) Irish practices were kept alive in the scriptorium at Lindisfarne. The copying of manuscripts proceeded according to the routine first brought from Iona by Aidan. During Eadfrith's rule Bede journeyed north to Lindisfarne from Jarrow. Later, Bede was to indicate his respect for the bishop by dedicating his biography of St. Cuthbert to him. Thanks to the colophon of the Lindisfarne Gospels we know of the part played by Bishop Eadfrith in preparing this Gospel Codex whose leaves proclaim the tenacity of the Irish hand in the scriptorium long after the Council of Whitby.[28] For three years after Eadfrith's death spiritual and intellectual life at Lindisfarne went undirected until the appointment of Ethelwold, abbot of Melrose, who had been trained at Lindisfarne, learning there the art of stone working. He was to raise a stone cross on whose face appeared Irish art motifs introduced to Northumbria in the time of Oswald and Aidan.[29] During his tenure (724–40), Ethelwold's *familia* witnessed the arrival of King Ceolwulf in 737, who had renounced an earthly kingdom plagued by unrest and discontent. With him Ceolwulf brought not only deeds to new lands mentioned previously, but an unlooked-for blessing—wine to be drunk at meals in place of the milk and water prescribed by Irish tradition.[30]

Under Bishop Cynewulf (740–80), the bond of amity between Lindisfarne and Bamburgh was sorely strained. Cynewulf chose to offer protection to Offa, a prince of royal blood seeking refuge at Lindisfarne from King Eadbert. The king's retainers dragged Offa from the altar and Cynewulf with him. At Eadbert's command Offa was executed and Bishop Cynewulf was imprisoned at Bamburgh for harboring a traitor.

The year 793 marked the first raid on Lindisfarne by Viking ravagers, news of which prompted Alcuin to express sympathy to the *familia* through Higbald, bishop until 802.[31] In one letter written after the catastrophe Alcuin makes his well-known reference to the inappropriateness of ecclesiastical interest in the sound of the harp and pagan songs (*carmina gentilium*), mentioning the name of Ingeld whose futile attack on Heorot is recalled by readers of *Beowulf*. What will happen to less eminent

monasteries, queries Alcuin, if God sees fit to bring down wrath
and retribution on Lindisfarne—the holy of holies—in the form
of pagan massacre and rapine?[32]

Among the English monasteries lying under threat of destruction in 793 were many that had been established by Aidan's
men sent out from Lindisfarne to "those provinces of the English
over which King Oswald reigned." Bede records that young and
old flocked to these churches to be instructed "in the studies and
observation of monastic rule," by Irishmen who had commenced
"with great devotion to preach the word of faith" (*H. E. III*, 3).[33]
Products of the zeal of Aidan and his disciples and successors,
these monasteries were evidence of the amicable relations between Bamburgh and Lindisfarne and of the lasting influence of
the Irish regimen imported from Iona. Therefore, it is important
to identify quickly the chief houses founded under the aegis of
Lindisfarne, and with it facing plunder and pillage in 793.

One such monastery was Lastingham in the North Riding of
Yorkshire, given (*circa* 648) to Bishop Cedd by Oswald's son,
Edilbald, king of Deira.[34] His father's friendship with Aidan
prompted Edilbald to grant land to Cedd for the founding of
Lastingham. Ordained at Lindisfarne, Cedd received from Aidan
his subsequent commission to preach to the East Saxons.

On the coast of the North Riding of Yorkshire, not far from
Lastingham, stood Whitby. Near the year 657 Oswy presented
land to a certain Hild in consequence of a vow she had made
to establish her own monastery.[35] To Whitby Hild brought a
spiritual routine practised at Hartlepool, on the coast of Durham,
where she had been visited by Aidan. From Whitby were to
come future bishops of York, Dorchester, and Hexham. There
also Caedmon, the inspired cowherd, sang his songs for Hild and
her copyists (*H. E. IV*, 24).[36]

Similar to Lastingham and Whitby was Ripon in the West
Riding of Yorkshire, a third monastery with Irish affiliations in
its founding tradition. Alchfrid (Oswy's son) gave Ripon to
Eata to build a monastery. Wilfrid was made abbot there before
661, and proceeded to send away both Eata and Cuthbert, who
had also been appointed monk there. According to Dugdale,

both men were sent away for refusing to observe the Easter date and canonical rites of the Roman church.[37] Up to the time of Wilfrid's arrival Irish customs were observed at Ripon under Cuthbert and Eata, both of whom had been instructed at Lindisfarne.

At Tynemouth in Northumbria, Edwin of Northumbria, between 617 and 633, erected a wooden building for nuns that was subsequently torn down by Oswald who raised a stone building in its place.[38]

Irish connections for the monastery of Gilling in Yorkshire are given by Bede: "Now the first bishop made in the province of the Marchmen, as well as of the Lindisfaras and of the Middle Englishmen, was . . . Diuma who died and was buried in the country of the Middle Englishmen: the second was Ceollach, who, leaving the charge of his bishopric yet living, returned to Scotland [Ireland]. Both these were Scottish [Irish] born. The third bishop was Trumhere, of English birth but fully instructed and ordained of the Scots [Irish], who was abbot of the monastery which is named Ingetlingum" (H. E. III, 24).[39]

Only twenty-two miles north of Lindisfarne across the Scottish border was Coldingham in Berwickshire, where Adamnan (not to be confused with the biographer of St. Columba) was proud of the harsh penance prescribed for him by a fellow Irish monk who had taken shelter there on his way to Ireland (H. E. IV, 25).

It was at Melrose in southeast Scotland that Cuthbert came under the tutelage of an Irishman named Boisil, "a priest of great virtues and of a prophetical spirit," according to Bede. Apprenticed to Boisil, Cuthbert became "his humble scholar, and learned of him both the knowledge of the Scriptures and examples of good works" (H. E. IV, 27).[40] Irish influence at Melrose is reflected in Bede's story of the vision of Drythelm, recounted to one of Bede's informants by Hemgils, one of Drythelm's fellow monks, himself "admitted to the priesthood which he honoured with his good works, being eminent in his degree, who remaineth yet alive, and in the isle of Ireland leading a solitary life supporteth his last days with coarse bread and cold water" (H. E.

V, 12).[41] On one of his visits to Melrose from Bamburgh, King Aldfrith (d. 705) had been entertained by Hemgils' story of Drythelm's vision of the other world.

The missionary work of St. Chad, sent out from Lindisfarne, resulted in the founding of the monastery at Barrow, near Hull in Yorkshire. Bede writes: " . . . king Wulfhere also gave unto him the land of 50 households to build a monastery in the place that is called Adbarwae, that is By the Wood, in the province of Lindsey, where until this day the steps of monastical life which Chad established there do yet remain" (*H. E.* IV, 3).[42]

Even at Crayke in Yorkshire Irish influence was felt. According to Dugdale, Crayke, near York, was originally a donation to St. Cuthbert at the hands of "Egfrid, King of the Northumbers."[43]

In addition to these prominent northern monasteries with Irish ties, to the south stood other famous houses with Irish elements in their founding traditions.[44] At Malmesbury, Glastonbury, and Abingdon, the routine of work and prayer was carried on in these times of great danger just as it was at Lindisfarne.

Alcuin's correspondents at Lindisfarne would inform him of further Viking depredations before his death in 804. During Egbert's episcopate (803–21) the Lindisfarne *familia* intermittently fled to Durham as enemy prows beached on Lindisfarne, their owners seeking more plunder. At some time during Egbert's uneasy tenure a poem entitled *Aedilvulfi Carmen* came from the hands of Ethelwulf, a monk trained at Lindisfarne[45] and possibly a member of the *familia* at Crayke. Addressed to the unfortunate Bishop Egbert, *Aedilvulfi Carmen* recites the trials undergone by previous leaders of Lindisfarne during the reign of the anti-clerical and tyrannical King Osred (705–16). Ethelwulf's account includes the story of one Eanmund, "dux nobilis natu et moribus," forced to flee the Bamburgh tyrant and take refuge in a monastery—perhaps Whitby, Melrose, or Coldingham. Impressed by the monastic life, Eanmund decided to establish a monastery of his own and accordingly wrote to Bishop Eadfrith, Bede's host at Lindisfarne, and to a Bishop Egbert (d. 729) who had gone to Ireland as a monk, making the pilgrimage for Christ (*H. E.* III, 27).[46] In accordance with advice received from Ead-

frith and Egbert, Eanmund built a monastery, at an unidentified
location, on the lines of Iona and Lindisfarne. In his service was
Ultan, an Irish scribe whose skill with stylus and brush was un-
matched. A fellow-Irishman named Cucuin wielded the hammer
in his soot-blackened hut, shaping hooks, pins, and pots for the
kitchen, and iron styluses for the school.[47]

By 793 we can look back to Aidan's arrival and see that the
Irish and their Northumbrian converts had demonstrated that
although Christ and Ingeld could not share the same hall, each
could hold sway in adjacent halls without imposing excessive
compromise or bloodshed on the other's followers. Despite occasional temporary breakdowns, a technique of "dispersion and
disconnection" that had typified the organization of the Irish
home monasteries in the fifth and sixth centuries proved work-
able at Lindisfarne and throughout Northumbria long after
635.[48]

Moreover, the brotherhood of the *familia* was not so completely unlike membership in the *comitatus,* particularly if a man's
chief was a pious Oswald or Aldfrith. For the thane who went
behind the monastic *vallum,* there was little to fear. Since a
King Ceolwulf could leave Bamburgh for Lindisfarne with little
hesitation, his thanes could do the same. In exchange for the
recurring violence of life in a war-band they could expect the
relative tranquility of the *familia* where strange and marvelous
deeds were performed with word and pen, where the feats of
the hero as told in *Judith, Andreas, Elene,* or *Christ* were to be
enjoyed vicariously.

As for hardship and danger, both monk and convert knew
much of both long before the Viking raiding parties appeared.
Verses of the Exeter Book reveal the effect which an eerie, solitary landscape must have had on the missionaries and pilgrims
who set out across it. Many had faced the flying hail and icy
spray that struck to the marrow of the *Seafarer* poet.[49] Certainly
since the era of Brendan and Columba, the Irish had known
the lot of the man who "of necessity [shall] travel on foot, upon
distant paths, and carry his food, walk through the rain, on the
dangerous soil of alien peoples" described in the *Fates of Men.*[50]

Irish missionaries and English converts had been exposed to the perils of wolf, bear, and boar related in the *Gnomic Verses*.[51] To both *familia* and *comitatus* the earthquakes and thunderstorms of the *Riddles* were all too real.[52]

Most important for this study is the fact that behind the *vallum* at Lindisfarne and the monasteries in its sphere of influence the convert was absorbed into a pattern of work, study, and prayer unchanged since its importation into Scotland and Northumbria by Columba and Aidan. It is to an examination of this regimen at its Irish source and an appraisal of its impact on that great Northumbrian king, Aldfrith, who ruled from 685 to 705, that we turn next.

Though he be cunning at carving cold stones,
though he be skilled at plying an axe,
though sweet his chant at songs,
I have heard that he who does not study is dull.

Martyrology of Oengus

*Chapter*

# III

## CHRIST'S KNIGHT, KING'S BISHOP, AND IRISH LEARNING IN THE SEVENTH CENTURY

Thanks to Bishop Adamnan, ninth abbot of Iona and Columba's biographer, we know that Iona's bread was baked by a *Sasanach* during the first years. More important, we learn from Adamnan's pen of his close friendship with King Aldfrith of Northumbria in the decades following the Council of Whitby.[1] Aldfrith's rule at Bamburgh (685–705) earned him this entry taken from a four-teenth-century manuscript of *Vita S. Cuthburgae*: "super modernos reges literarum eruditus scientia."[2] His father, Oswy, had come under Iona's protection before taking control of his kingdom, and the half-Irish Aldfrith had been an exile at Iona and in Ireland itself, perhaps because of his illegitimacy. The Irish annalists of the *Three Fragments* hail him as "the wondrous sage, Adamnan's pupil." Bede believed that Aldfrith had spent time in Ireland to gratify his love of literature and he calls him "very well learned in the Scriptures (*H. E.* IV, 26). His brother, Ecg-frith, had offered him a bishopric which he refused, believing himself unworthy. To Alcuin, Aldfrith was "idem rex simul atque magister"—the philosopher-king.[3]

Perhaps at Clonard or Clonmacnoise Aldfrith learned the art

of poetry. Three separate compositions in Irish are attributed to
this Northumbrian king, including gnomic verses[4] and a poem
on the beheading of John the Baptist. If Aldfrith was the author
of the third work, a multi-stanza poem, he may have discovered
to be true most of what Northumbrian tradition and legend had
ascribed to Ireland since before Aidan's arrival in 635. Aldfrith
and earlier Northumbrians, mentioned by Bede as visiting Ireland "in the time of the bishops Finan and Colman" (*H. E.* III,
27), saw the fruits of Patrick's, Columba's, and Brendan's labors
in the monasteries at Armagh, Durrow, and Clonfert.[5] With apparent vivid recollection, Aldfrith strikes off stanzas in honor of
his Irish hosts:

> .   .   .   .   .   .
>
> I found in each province
> Of the five provinces of Ireland,
> Both in Church and State,
> Much of food—much of raiment.
>
> .   .   .   .   .
>
> I found in each great church
> Whether internal, on shore or island,
> Learning, wisdom, devotion to God,
> Holy welcome, and protection.
>
> I found the lay monks
> Of alms the active advocates,
> And in proper order of them
> The Scriptures without corruption.
>
> .   .   .   .   .
>
> I found the aged of strict morals,
> The historians recording truth;
> Each good, each benefit that I have sung,
> In Ireland I have seen.[6]

Aldfrith marks the presence of "women of worth," wheat, and
honey in abundance. In Munster he finds "poets well-skilled in
music and measure." Ulster has "hardy warriors" and Boyle
boasts "weapons bright, and horsemen bold." All these sights did
"Fair Flann Fina, son of Osswy" confirm for himself in "Inisfail
the Fair."[7]

In this chapter our particular aim will be to supply details from contemporary sources verifying the monasteries as places where Aldfrith and his countrymen had found "Learning, wisdom, devotion to God,/ Holy welcome, and protection." We may thereby shed light also on the nature of the intellectual regimen brought to Iona by Columba and instituted at Lindisfarne by Aidan—a regimen that produced lasting monuments in vellum and stone to Irish influence in Northumbria.

From Patrick's time, the Irish abbot headed an ecclesiastical clan that drew membership from adjacent tribal groups, thus giving many members of the *familia* a common lineage.[8] His title and responsibilities were apparently handed at his death to his nearest qualified descendant.[9] On this point ancient Irish laws seem explicit: "The Church of the Tribe of the Saint. That is, the tribe of the Saint shall succeed in the Church as long as there shall be a person fit to be an abbot, . . . of the tribe of the saint, even though there should be but a psalm-singer of these, it is he that will obtain the abbacy. Where this is not the case, it is to be given to the tribe of the land until a person fit to be an abbot, of the tribe of the saint, shall be found."[10]

The abbot was assisted by a vice-abbot, the cellarer, the guestmaster, and a bishop.[11] Under the non-diocesan organization of the Irish church, the bishop administered rituals and sacraments, whereas the abbot controlled the day-to-day activities of the *familia*.[12] Clustered behind the wall were kitchen, cells, workshop, guesthouse, scriptorium, school, and church. Northumbrian visitors to Ireland in the seventh century often knelt in stone and timber churches that would suffer at the hands of Scandinavian invaders after 800.[13] Many monasteries like Clonard, Clonfert, Bangor, and Clonmacnoise boasted ornate wooden churches like this one, described by an eighth-century inmate of Kildare:

I must not be silent concerning the miracle at the restoration of the church in which rest the glorious bodies of bishop Conlaeth and the virgin saint Brigid, on the right and left of the decorated altar, deposited in monuments decorated with various embellishments of gold and silver and precious stones, with crowns of gold and silver hung above them. For, owing to the increase in the number of the

Faithful, and their being of both sexes, the church occupied a wide area and was raised to a towering height, and was adorned with painted pictures. It had within three spacious oratories, separated by plank partitions, under the one roof of the greater house, wherein one partition, decorated and painted with figures, and covered with linen hangings, extended along the breadth of the eastern part of the church from one wall of the church to the other. Which partition has at its ends two doors. Through the one door, placed on the right-hand side, the chief bishop enters the sanctuary accompanied by his regular school, and by those who are appointed to the holy ministry of offering sacred and dominical sacrifices.[14]

The Northumbrians mingled with throngs of ecclesiastics ranging in number from one hundred to three thousand members. The visitors prayed, worked, broke bread, and read with monks, many of whom came to the monasteries after having been selected for religious training in boyhood by their parents.[15] We read that St. Declan at the age of seven "was taken from his parents and friends and fosterers to be sent to study as Colman had ordained."[16]

In order that he might feed the monastic family and current visitors at the guest-house (Ir. *tech n-oiged*), the abbot exercised his right to claim every first calf and every first lamb of each year, and the first gathering of the produce of the fields.[17] Provender yielded from this source was supplemented by the labors of working brothers under the abbot's command.[18] Only thus was it possible to feed the large communities mentioned in the hagiographical works.

In the monastic school was conducted the vital work of learning the formation of letters through the use of implements and materials like those discovered at the site of the monastery of Nendrum at Inishmee in Strangford Loch near Bangor, Ireland. At what might well have been one of Aldfrith's "island monasteries," about thirty tablets of slate and stone survive, inscribed with designs made by recruits for the scriptorium. Three tablets had been used for lettering practice. One shows efforts to form the letter *m* in runic characters, another is inscribed with experimental *e*'s, and the third has part of the alphabet traced on its surface.[19] Other tablets show attempts at executing ornament

including border designs, circles, and spirals. Iron styluses taken
from the site are described as being "all over five inches in
length, from the flat disc to the point, which indicates that they
were made to fit the hand of an adult."[20]

Evidence concerning the establishment of Iona reveals a simi-
larity between the writing instruments used there and those
found at Nendrum. Adamnan, in a treatise on the holy sites of
Christianity, mentions wax tablets: "Cuius mihi formam in tabula
cerata ipse depinxit."[21] In his biography of St. Columba, he
notes tablets used in the Iona scriptorium: "At vero hoc audiens
Colcius tempus et horam in tabula describens."[22] Tablets are re-
ferred to also in the life of St. Maedoc (d. 632): "Sciensque uir
Dei causam ipsius, possuit ceraculum suum super cornua ipsius."[23] Again there is evidence of their existence during the
period of English visitation: " . . . et libris stylo ipsius descrip-
tis."[24] In Irish hagiography the tablets are called *clar ciartha
scribtha*[25] and in the Latin life of St. Kenneth (d. 600) appears:
"Porta tecum in signum 'illi' graffium istud, quod in aere ex pallio
eius cadens reliquit."[26]

Wax tablets and iron or wooden styluses were put into the
hands of Irish and Northumbrian pupils showing aptitude for
the scribal routine. Of these students the most skillful were later
assigned to the scriptoria where parchment and vellum were
substituted for tablets, and pen and inkhorn for styluses.

In the scriptorium Aldfrith observed a routine prescribed since
the sixth century. The main functions of the scriptorium in Ireland or Northumbria were to supply textbooks for the monastic
school, service-books for the church and monastic community,
and documents of a more general type for the library.[27] Adamnan
tells of Columba's being interrupted while writing with intense
concentration at Iona. The saint paused to extend a blessing, his
outstretched hand still holding the pen.[28] Adamnan relates also
a humorous incident involving Columba and a spilled inkhorn
at Iona: "On another day a shout was given on the other side of
the Sound of the Iouan island [Sound of Iona]; the saint hearing the shout, as he was sitting in his little hut, which was made
of planks, said 'The man who is shouting beyond the Sound is

not of very sharp wit, for when he is here to-day he will upset my inkhorn and spill the ink.' Diormit, his minister, hearing this, stood a little in front of the door, and waited for the arrival of this troublesome guest, in order to save the inkhorn. But for some cause or other he had soon to leave his place, and after his departure the unwelcome guest arrived; in his eager haste to kiss the saint, he upset the inkhorn with the hem of his garment and spilled the ink."[29]

The use of manuscripts for study and imitation in the scribal workroom by the Irish and their English students is revealed in the *vitae* of St. Moinu, St. Lasrian, and St. Kevin of Glendalough.[30] Used for scribal instruction, these manuscripts lay in satchels slung from pegs on the walls of the scriptorium. Fashioned by artisans of the *familia* from heavy leather, the satchels were embossed with abstract and intricate interlacement with no beginning and no end.

Abundant evidence from Irish-Latin saints' lives emphasizes the prominence given the scribe and his handiwork in the Irish monastery. Two episodes from different *vitae* describe the practice whereby scribes were loaned to neighboring scriptoria.[31] Manuscripts, as well as their makers, were exchanged freely. One seventh-century biography gives the following account: "Alio quoque tempore Lasriano exeunti in quadam remota terra a suis occurrunt sibi clerici quidam, quorum libros respiciens, v[nu]m ex eis scribere uoluit; pennam uero qua librum scribere posset minime habebat. Eleuatis ergo manibus ad aues supra se in aere uolantes, pen[n]a una cecidit, cum qua librum desideratum scripsit."[32]

At Mayo where transplanted Englishmen preserved the rule of Columba after leaving Northumbria with Colman in 664, time was reserved for the improvement of scribal skills originally learned at Lindisfarne: "Post eius uero obitum sanctus Adampnanus Maionensem ecclesiam per septem annos indefesse rexit, claustrales in caritate perfecta instruens, uolumina conscribi faciens, atque manu propria librum quatuor euangeliorum scribens, campanas etiam ad reuerenciam ecclesie fabrifaciens."[33]

Other documents reinforce the testimony of the *vitae* concern-

ing the importance of the scribe. In the *Martyrology of Oengus*
we read: "Now Cairnech the Bald was the scribe of Ciaran of
Saiger. 'Tis he that wrote the wonderful manuscript, namely
*Ciaran's Journey,* with its many various illuminations, and this
book still remains in Saiger."[34] In reference to his own scholarly
quest, Oengus writes: "Ireland's host of books, whose troop is
wise, we have searched multitudes of them, the martyrologies
of the men of the Gaels."[35] A clue concerning the value of manuscripts in Ireland is provided in an account of Columba's visit
with a scholar-monk: "He was a master of study and jurisprud-
ence and history and poetry. To him once came Colum cille
[Columba] and he hid his books from the latter, and Colum
cille left a word on his books, i.e., 'May that as to which thou
showest inhospitality be of no profit after thee.' And this has been
fulfilled, for still the books remain and no one studies them."[36]

Irish annals reflect the respect accorded the scribe in the monasteries even through the era of Scandinavian terror. Entries
like the following from the *Annals of Ulster* relate the deaths of
"eminent and excellent" scribes including "Ceile, comarb of
Comgall, a scribe and anchorite . . . [who] rested happily at
Rome, on his pilgrimage."[37]

But it was more than a willingness to submit to the tedious
routine of the scribe and copyist that drew Bede's "nobles as
well as common sort" to Ireland. Had the English yearned only
for greater asceticism and self-denial, Lindisfarne's abbots, nota-
bly St. Cuthbert, could have saved them the journey by prescrib-
ing more rigorous rules to follow in the Northumbrian houses.
In part the migration was the natural result of a happy cultural
blending process between Ireland and Northumbria that had
the Iona establishment for its model. For some there was the
promise of hospitality, the prospect of respite from civil turmoil,
and pleasant months spent with a people whose spiritual representatives they had come to know and respect. But others, like
Aldfrith, undertook the journey to Clonmacnoise, Bangor, Nendrum, Mayo, Clonard, or Clonfert to avail themselves of a store
of learning only slightly depleted by the demands made on it
from Iona, Lindisfarne, and the Continent.[38] The nature of this

learning is described in a letter from Aldhelm to a certain Eahfrith, after the latter's return to Britain from a six-year stay in
an Irish monastery.[39] Aldhelm, about whose debt to Irish
learning we should like to know more, posed this question wist-
fully: "Why, say I, should Ireland, whither students, shipborne,
flock together in summer, why should Ireland be exalted by some
ineffable privilege . . . ? The fields of Ireland are rich in learn-
ers, and green with the pastural numerosity of students, as the
pivots of the pole quiver with the vibrations of the glittering
constellations."[40] Elsewhere in this missive Aldhelm alludes to
the study of grammar, geometry, physics, and the allegorical
interpretation of the Scriptures in the Irish schools.[41] Under-
standably, the study of Holy Writ was the dominant intellectual
activity in the monasteries visited by Aldfrith. Approaching the
Bible as a volume of enigmas to be solved in good time were
individual scholars at Clonard and Clonfert whose work must
have been known to the Northumbrians. The original impetus
for this exegetical discipline had been provided, as we noted in
Chapter I, by the influx of learning from British monasteries in
the fifth century and the arrival of Gaulish missionaries and
refugees from the Continent.[42]

By Aldfrith's time the steps necessary to the training of an
exegete were firmly established. First came the learning of Latin,
followed by the reading of the fragmented works of Latin
authors. Theology, including dogma, moral and canon law, and
ritual were next taken up. Finally came the study of Scripture.[43]
For the student who achieved excellence in the last-named
phase there awaited the title of Doctor of the Letter (Ir. *sui
littre*), an honor possibly equal to that accorded the master of
native learning (Ir. *ollam*).[44] Many saints' lives contain references to this rigorous discipline. In the life of St. Aed (d. 589)
we read of that saint's preoccupation with "litteras et scripturas,"[45] and from the life of St. Cronan of Ross Cree (d. 626)
comes "ut sanctas legeret scripturas, et disciplinam ecclesiasticam
a sanctis patribus disceret."[46] Certain of the Northumbrian guests
could look forward to instruction in the reading of Scripture
leading to the accumulation of special knowledge (Ir. *legend*).

The effort devoted to *legend* is underscored by Roger: "Étudier les lettres sacrées, trouver, dans l'exemple des saints, un encouragement à s'élever de sacrifice en sacrifice jusqu'à la sainteté, connaître les règles et la discipline ecclésiastique, et apprendre ainsi le chemin de la vie, tel était l'objet proposé à leur ardeur. Au premier rang de leurs occupations se trouve la lecture sacrée. On lit à Clonard, on lit à Bangor, on lit à Iona. Et la lecture, pour les Irlandais, ce n'est pas seulement réciter les psaumes et les hymnes. . . . La lecture sacrée comprend l'interprétation de l'Écriture elle-même. Faut-il croire, pour cette raison, que l'enseignement des lettres ait été, dès ce moment, organisé dans les centres importants?"[47]

In pursuing the aim of *legend* zealous monks and students gave close scrutiny to literature of the late Latin period on the Continent, remnants of which had been preserved in Irish monastic schools since their founding.[48] Doubtless, some excursions into the realm of pagan rhetoric were pushed more vigorously than St. Jerome would have wished.[49] For the most part, however, those documents with which Northumbrians became acquainted were of native provenance.[50] From St. Brendan's Clonfert in 632 came a treatise on the dating of Easter by Cummian, who draws on Jerome, Cyprian, Augustine, and Gregory the Great, in addition to the Bible, in presenting his case.[51] Known also to the Northumbrian visitors was a tract entitled *De mirabilibus sanctae scripturae,* written in three parts near 655 by an unknown author who goes by the modest title, the "Irish Augustine."[52] He writes first of the law to the death of Moses; second, of the prophets; third, of the New Testament. With naive solemnity he explains the metamorphosis of Lot's wife by stating that she turned to salt because there had been an abnormal development of the "saltable element" in her body. A more flattering reflection of the Irish Augustine's intellectual powers is his commentary on the Deluge where he lists the animals found in Ireland in his time and expresses the belief that islands such as Ireland were formed by the action of the sea separating them from the mainland.

At Finnian's Clonard, the monk Aileran had produced his

*Interpretatio mystica progenitorum domini Jesu Christi,* with its heavy reliance on allegorical interpretation, a work known to the Northumbrian visitors at Iona and the home monasteries.[53] Both the Irish Augustine, Aileran, and their lesser contemporaries fostered Scriptural glosses, commentaries, explications, and exegeses unequalled in places of learning until our time! Surely they rest peacefully knowing they cannot be accused of having wasted their efforts on a trivial composition.

Whereas these seventh-century exegetes and their disciples spun out their explications undisturbed, working abbots and bishops such as Adamnan of Iona had precious little time for writing.[54] Yet, despite the demands of his office, Adamnan found time to finish, in addition to the biography of Columba, a treatise on holy sites, and possibly a series of scholia on the *Eclogues* and *Georgics* of Virgil. At hand for his study at Iona were stylistic exemplars in the form of partial texts of classical pagan works.[55] In his life of Columba appear probable influences from the *Aeneid* and the *Georgics*:

| *Virgil* | *Vita Columbae* |
|---|---|
| Georg. III, 439; Aen. II, 475: et linguis micat ore trisulcis | III, 23: viperarum venena trisulcarum linguarum |
| Aen. II, 372: verbis compellat amicis | II, 35: pacificisque verbis blande . . . compellat |
| Aen. V, 125: tumidis submersum . . . fluctibus | I, 1: Tumores quoque . . . fluctuum |
| Aen. V, 432: aeger anhelitus | II, 33: anhelantem aegra reliquit suspiria |
| Aen. VI, 699: largo fletu simul ora rigabat | II, 42: faciem lacrymis ubertim irrigans[56] |

How well the scholarship of Adamnan and the seventh-century Irish exegetes known to the Northumbrians compared with that of their brilliant ninth-century successors who flourished at the court of Charles the Great is debatable.[57] There seems no doubt, however, that the groundwork for the sensitive Irish handling of classical literature as an aid and support to grammatical and Scriptural study was laid as early as the sixth century at monasteries like Clonard and Bangor. Nor can we fail to believe that members of the community at Iona and Lindisfarne had access to shelves holding such intriguing titles as those appearing in the ninth-century Codex Vossianus from the scriptorium at Fleury, a center of Irish monastic culture on the Continent. Aileran, the Irish Augustine, and undoubtedly Adamnan himself had learned *grammatica* with the help of such documents as *Disticha Catonis,* selections from Martial, part of Isidore's chapter on grammar from the *Etymologiae,* and Christian poems including a work on Jonah and Sodom ascribed to Tertullian.[58] A similar ninth-century manuscript, Codex Bernensis 363, compiled by an Irish cleric at Milan contains a commentary by Servius on the *Bucolics, Georgics,* and *Aeneid,* on poems of Horace, and on extracts from Ovid's *Metamorphoses.*[59] From the catalog of the library at St. Gall, founded as a result of the mission of St. Columbanus to the Continent in the sixth century, come titles of Irish-written manuscripts treating of figures of speech and versification in the form of a dialogue between master and pupil, and of a copy of Priscian's *De Grammatica* with Irish glosses written in Ireland and brought to the Continent.[60] Like Columbanus, whose own early training in Latin verse forms at Bangor is reflected in manuscripts at Lorsch, Reichenau, and Bobbio, Adamnan and Aldfrith knew their classical authors.[61] It is inconceivable that Aldfrith could have become known as "Erin's chief sage of learning" and "a man most learned in all ways" without having assimilated in Ireland writings of a type that were well known in certain centers of Irish culture on the Continent as early as the sixth century.[62] It is equally unlikely that Aldfrith and Adamnan did not share the known interest of their time in church history.[63]

The compilations in ninth-century Continental manuscripts hark back to earlier Irish interests and sources of learning of the fifth through eighth centuries.[64] The anthologies at Fleury and St. Gall throw light on the cordial reconciliation between

Christian belief and pagan culture that was a part of the scene surveyed by Aldfrith and his countrymen. What was read, studied, and taught at Irish monasteries was read, studied, and taught at Iona and Lindisfarne, although perhaps on a more modest scale. It would be wrong to think of the scriptorium and library at Iona and Lindisfarne as producing and possessing only liturgical documents, magnificent as are the Book of Kells and the Gospels of Lindisfarne. Humble missals, hymnals, and Psalters as well as elaborately decorated Gospel texts were copied in the scriptorium, but also there were important glosses, grammars, and fragments of the classical heritage to be read, studied, and transcribed.

Adamnan's own *Vita S. Columbae* and *De locis sanctis* prove that training in Latin letters could be substantial in a seventh-century Irish monastery. His pride in the latter work led Adamnan to dedicate it to Aldfrith and deliver it into the king's own hands at Bamburgh.[65] There it was accepted graciously by a half-Irish Northumbrian king, a patron of learning who was himself learned, thanks to his Irish residence. Aldfrith's every effort, as far as we can ascertain, was to maintain a kingdom resembling in many respects that "Inisfail the Fair" sketched in verse of his own proud making.[66] Happily, unlike Charles the Great, a ruler also surrounded by Irish learning and scholars, Aldfrith found no need to place his slate beneath his pillow at Bamburgh that he might practice forming his letters in the middle of the night. His eyes and hands had long since become used to the sight and feel of vellum, pen, and ink.

I send my little dripping pen·unceasingly
over an assemblage of books of great beauty,
to enrich the possessions of men of art
whence my hand is weary with writing.
From a poem ascribed to St. Columba

*Chapter*
# IV

## THE IRISH SCRIBE
## AND THE INSULAR HAND

In 1609, Federico Cardinal Borromeo, Archbishop of Milan, founded the Ambrosian Library. Among its initial treasures was one manuscript already close to one thousand years old. As he turned its leaves, however, the keeper of the Cardinal's manuscripts may well have wondered why this diminutive book had not been left at Bobbio where, as tradition held, there lay a host of well-thumbed, dog-eared missals, hymnals, and similar workaday products from forgotten monasteries in a far-off land —Ireland, was it? Never mind. He would find a niche, an unobtrusive corner to which its drabness recommended it, for he had noted with regret the absence of colored initials and rich ornament in its seventy-two folios. Thus, for over a century it stood on a shelf, its canticles, hymns, collects, and versicles enclosed between sewn sheets of limp parchment, a church service-book written between 680 and 691 in the scriptorium at Bangor founded by St. Comgall, friend and contemporary of Columba of Iona. Paleographers know it now as the Antiphonary of Bangor, a prime example of an Irish manuscript from a seventh-century scriptorium. To church historians it is the sole documentary source for the liturgical practices of the Irish monastic church.[1] For this study, the Antiphonary is all the above and

more—visible evidence of the discipline of the scriptorium in the
time of Adamnan and Aldfrith, corroboration for the statements
in the annals and saints' *vitae* concerning the status and duties
of the copyist, and a convenient place to begin tracing the story
of the supremacy of the Lindisfarne scriptorium before and after
the Council of Whitby.

Even had the Cardinal not removed the Antiphonary to Milan
for safekeeping, thereby assuring its publication in complete
form in 1770 by Muratori, a tireless Italian archivist, we would
not have remained ignorant for long of the Irish achievement
in the art of writing—itself "an expression and a register of the
spirit" informing its own age.[2] The steps in the emergence of a
singular style of script that was to last for over five hundred
years are to be seen today in hundreds of documents. Chilled
stiff fingers copied them at Lindisfarne, Iona, and Bangor, and
on the Continent of St. Gall, Bobbio, Reichenau, and Fleury,
from the seventh through the tenth centuries.

Adamnan wrote that for the father of Iona never an hour
passed "without study, or prayer, or writing."[3] As death ap-
proached, Columba "sat in his hut transcribing the Psalter";[4] he
had found time to examine for errors a transcription of the
Psalter done by one of the Iona *familia*.[5] Despite an occasional
candidate seemingly unable to form anything but a wretched
scrawl on his practice tablet, the places in the scriptorium were
kept filled.[6] Yet, too often a man of Bede's stature had to be his
own shorthand writer and copyist.[7]

The temptation to scribble a complaint or comment in manuscript margins was overpowering. "I am very cold," writes one
scribe. "The parchment is rough . . . ," laments another. "New
parchment, bad ink. O I say nothing more," cries a third.[8]
Errors are frequent. In the Antiphonary, wrong genders, omitted
letters, titles, and verses testify that the task of transcription
might be carried on in a mechanical way by men not always
sure with Latin letters.[9] But the impact of their errors and
omissions diminishes as rapidly as the total accomplishment of
the Irish and Northumbrian scribes can be measured. At work in
the scriptoria was that same aggressive and resolute independ-

ence of spirit and willingness to innovate that we marked in earlier chapters dealing with missionary and intellectual activity. This is not to imply, however, that the seemingly prosaic manuscript whose presence in the Ambrosiana may have vexed the Cardinal's librarian owed no debt to the Continent. As we shall see presently, even the Book of Kells and the Gospels of Lindisfarne may be beholden in a small way to the wall inscriptions uncovered from the dust of Pompeii and Herculaneum, and the messages inscribed on the Catacombs' dank walls.

Let us mark the rise of certain Latin scripts prior to Ireland's Christianization, trace the subsequent development of two distinctive Irish hands, and ascertain the place of the Antiphonary in this development. The earliest fragments of Latin writing found at Pompeii are written in a hand consisting of capitals tending toward cursive. A glance at Sample A, Figure 1, shows this hand to be the archaic alphabet written carelessly, sometimes on walls in the form of announcements with brush, and sometimes scrawled with charcoal, chalk, or a stylus on a variety of materials.[10] Irregularity in size and position of the letters is due mainly to the media used. Such a cursive hand formed the basis for the national hands of Italy, Spain, and the Frankish kingdom in the Middle Ages. A second Latin hand, popular in the first and second centuries, belongs in the category called "majuscule" (large writing in the upper case). One kind of this majuscule writing was the *Capitalis Quadrata,* or square capital style of uniform height between two parallel lines. Alongside the *Capitalis Quadrata* existed another majuscule hand, the *Capitalis Rustica,* best described as an irregular alphabet typified by narrower letters and thinner strokes, as seen in Sample B, Figure 1.

The uncial hand, also majuscule, is the third type of Latin writing important to this study. In Sample C, Figure 1, note that the uncial script simplified the *Capitalis* scripts by rounding the angles of certain letters. This tendency for straight lines to become curves produced a hand which combined the beauty and regularity of capitals with the rapidity of the cursive.

The earliest Continental specimen of the uncial hand is a fourth-century manuscript of Cicero's *De Republica* in the Vatican library. Another is the fifth-century Livy manuscript in the Imperial Library of Vienna.[11] Chief characteristics of the uncial hand as seen in these manuscripts are bold sweeping curves in the round letters; small bows in *b*, *p*, and *r*; the high-set bar of *e*; and the short cross-stroke of *t*. At least one sixth-century Gospel manuscript, preserved in the library at St. Gall, shows uncial letters possessing the above traits.

The fourth Latin hand of importance here is the semi-uncial, developing simultaneously with the uncial from capital cursive perhaps as early as the third century. When writing had to be done frequently and rapidly, majuscule writing evolved slowly into the more connected and less formal minuscule script (small letters in the lower case). Actually, there is no perceptible boundary-line between the majuscule and minuscule scripts. Although at first, both majuscule and minuscule types appear in the same Latin manuscripts, by the end of the fifth century most majuscule forms had disappeared. This Continental semi-uncial, brought to Ireland by missionaries and refugee scholars in the fifth and sixth centuries, evolved into the distinctive minuscule of the Antiphonary of Bangor.

The sixth-century Continental scribe copying a line from St. Augustine in the semi-uncial hand of Sample D, Figure 1, did so because he found this half-printed style of writing more adaptable to the arduous task of transcription than the labored movements required of the pure uncial. To compare this sample of the Continental semi-uncial with the cursive inscription from the walls of Pompeii in Sample A, is to see the attractiveness which the new hand must have held for scribes of Italy and southern France who developed it. Perhaps the finest illustration of this Continental semi-uncial that would give rise to the Irish hand is seen in Sample E, Figure 1, from a manuscript at Monte Cassino written before 569. Numerous Continental semi-uncial manuscripts of the type seen in Sample E suggest that the semi-uncial script was among the first of the hands seen in manuscripts carried to Ireland from Gaul.

There has been lengthy consideration by paleographers of the origin of the distinctive semi-uncial hand developed at Clonard,

FIGURE 1–Continental and Irish Hands. [*Continued on facing page*]

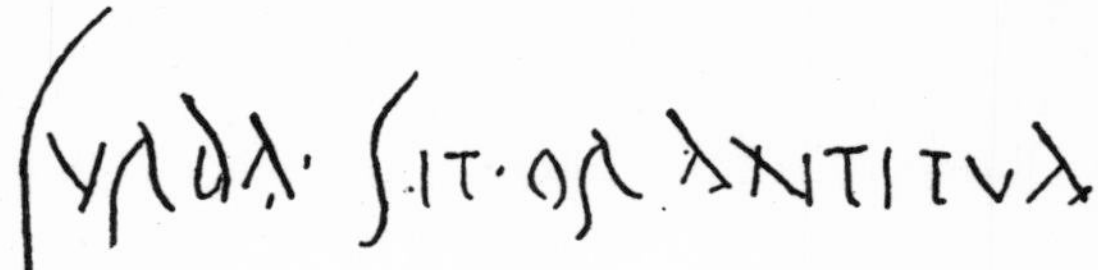

*ʃyʌðʌ· ʃiτ·oʌ ʌɴτιτυʌ*

A–Cursive hand as seen in Pompeian wall inscription–1st century. After Thompson, *Handbook*, p. 206.

Surda sit oranti tua [ianua laxa ferenti]

**TALIBUSIINSIDIISP**

B–Rustic Capital hand as seen in Vatican manuscript of Virgil of the fourth century. After Maurice Prou, *Manuel de Paléographie* (Paris, 1892), p. 17.

TALIBUS IINSIDIIS P

*a ð e ʃ h m ɋ τ u*

C–Uncial characters. After Prou, *Manuel*, p. 20.

A D E G H M Q T V

*ʜoɴcoȝɴouiɴiʀipeɴlegem·*

D–Continental semi-uncial hand as seen in manuscript from library at Orleans. After Prou, *Manuel*, p. 23.

non cognovi nisi per legem

aboleret· natuſerʒoe

*E*–Continental semi-uncial hand as seen in manuscript of Biblical commentary at Monte Cassino before 569. After Thompson, *Handbook*, p. 202.

aboleret natus ergo e

curmeurſupá·uepitdemaa

*F*–Irish round semi-uncial (latter seventh century) as seen in fragment of Trinity College Gospel manuscript. After Thompson, *Handbook*, p. 238.

[ami]cus meus supervenit de via a[d me]

ſeac· Se ıpsum ꞃoꞃp

*G*–Irish semi-uncial as seen in Book of Kells. After Thompson, *Handbook*, p. 239.

fecit. Se ipsum non p

*H*–English adaptation of Irish semi-uncial hand as seen in Lindisfarne Gospels. After Thompson, *Handbook*, p. 246.

Beati qui lugunt

laeꞇꞇiaꝃcauꝲaꝺ& ꝼꝺum.uꞇ

*I*–English pointed hand from manuscript of Bede's *Historia Ecclesiastica* (*circa* 730), University Library, Cambridge. After Thompson, *Handbook*, p. 249.

laetitae causa decretum ut

Bangor, Nendrum, Moville, and other monasteries visited by Northumbrians.[12] One theory holds that the Irish scribes had opportunity to copy both uncial and semi-uncial Continental hands appearing in manuscripts carried by missionaries arriving from the Continent and by Irish ecclesiastics returning from British monasteries in the sixth century. Also it is likely that exemplars in the majuscule hand were available when manuscript preparation was first undertaken.[13]

At any rate, the round Irish semi-uncial hand seems closely related to Roman semi-uncial writing in fifth- and sixth-century manuscripts from monasteries in France and Italy. Sample F, Figure 1, shows one of the oldest examples of this Irish script taken from a fragment of the Gospels in Trinity College, Dublin, and dated, like the Antiphonary of Bangor, close to the end of the seventh century. We shall meet this round Irish hand again in the Cathach (Psalter) ascribed to St. Columba of Iona. Evolving from this working book-hand of the Irish scriptoria of the seventh and eighth centuries there came a sumptuous ornamental hand shown in Sample G, Figure 1, from the Book of Kells.[14] In addition to the round semi-uncial, the Irish scriptoria developed a second, minuscule script. This is the so-called pointed hand, "a modification of the round hand, with the same forms of letters subject to lateral compression and drawn out into points or hair-lines."[15] It is this pointed hand which is used in the Antiphonary of Bangor, Figure 2.

Thus by the year of Aidan's mission to Bamburgh the round semi-uncial hand, a modification of the Roman semi-uncial, was well established in Irish scriptoria, including Iona.[16] Contemporaneous with it was the pointed hand. Both hands represent innovations and departures from the Continental semi-uncial permitted scribes happily isolated since the fifth century from Continental strife. Both hands were installed in the Lindisfarne scriptorium and both had been brought to a high degree of perfection in monasteries that played host to Aldfrith and his countrymen.

The fruits of Irish scribal tutelage are instantly obvious in the Gospels of Lindisfarne, prepared, according to its colophon, at

Lindisfarne by Bishop Eadfrith and others *circa* 700. Sample H, Figure 1, shows the debt of the Northumbrian ornamental round semi-uncial to its Irish prototype as do the Gospels of the monastery of St. Augustine at Canterbury, the Durham Cassiodorus, the Epinal Glossary, and several charters. Irish-trained scribes also mastered the pointed hand of the Irish scriptoria as seen in Sample I, Figure 1, taken from a manuscript of Bede's *Historia Ecclesiastica,* written not long after 730, probably at Echternach or a similar Anglo-Saxon colony on the Continent. In English scriptoria the pointed hand was used almost exclusively for documents, assuming definitely recognizable regional characteristics in Kentish, Mercian, and Wessex charters written in the eighth and ninth centuries.[17]

The Irish round hand, called by Lowe and others, "Irish majuscule," and the Irish pointed hand, "Irish minuscule," together with the corresponding English hands developed under Irish influence, will command our attention in the balance of this chapter and the next. From scriptoria at Bangor, Iona, and Lindisfarne came manuscripts like the Antiphonary of Bangor executed with skill by Irish scribes and their English students. Little did the Cardinal's librarian at Milan in 1609 realize that in his keeping lay one of the keys to an explanation of a paleographical phenomenon, fascinating both in its own right and as new evidence, taken with that of annals, chronicles, saints' lives, and church dedications, substantiating the intimate cultural tie between Dark-Age Ireland and Britain.

As the discipline of paleography gained stature close to the turn of this century, scholars paid new heed to manuscripts like the Antiphonary.[18] No longer did its unimpressive size (nine inches by seven inches) or its lack of rich ornament conspire to keep it in obscurity. Its authentic antiqueness, attested to by the final entry in a list of Bangor's abbots included in its folios, made it significant. Its obviously non-Continental hand that had eluded precise designation since the ninth century, being known first as *Scriptura Scotica,* later as *Scriptura Saxonica,* caught the eye. Although the manuscript boasted no colophon, the Antiphonary's scribe had left his imprint in other ways. His hand frequently

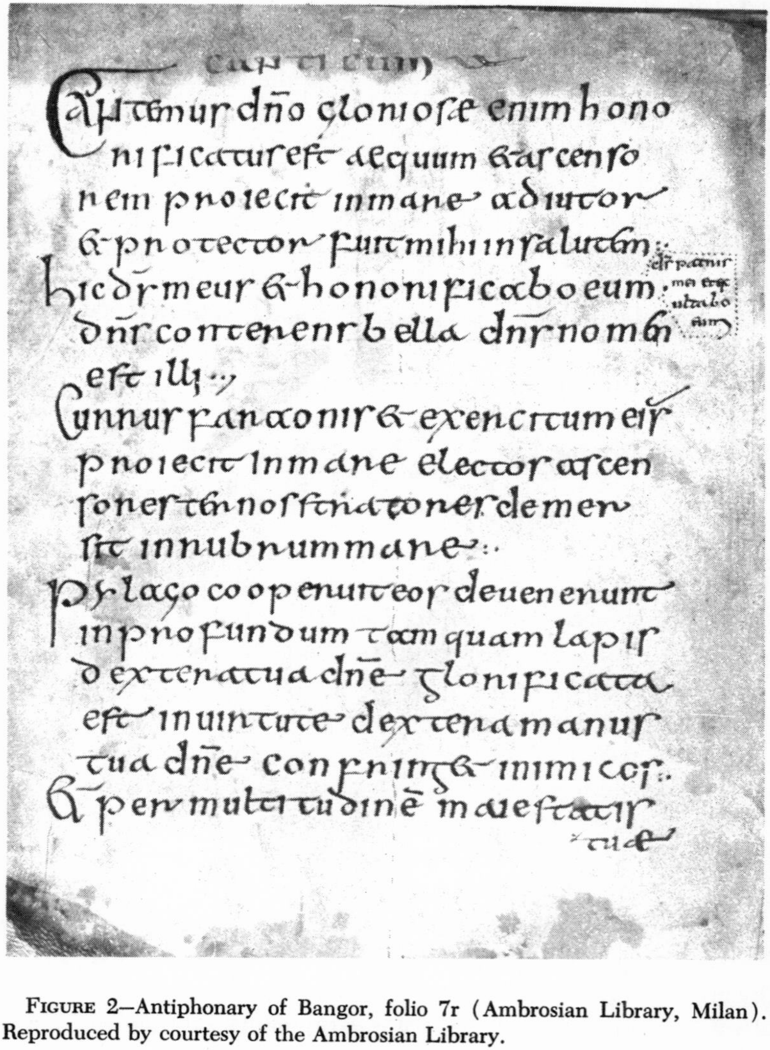

FIGURE 2—Antiphonary of Bangor, folio 7r (Ambrosian Library, Milan).
Reproduced by courtesy of the Ambrosian Library.

shaped a very open *p* or *q*. Some capitals he wrote three inches high, whereas others are as small as three-eighths of an inch. Often large capitals are followed by one, two, or three smaller capitals tapering off gradually in size.[19] The letter *a* is written sometimes with a deep downward flourish as the last letter in a line,[20] again with a high upward flourish over the line.[21] Before *m* and *n* the scribe may raise *i* above the line.[22] Although usually separated, the *ae* diphthong is occasonally combined,[23] whereas the *o* and *e* of the diphthong *oe* are always written separately.

Far more important than one scribe's idiosyncracies, however, were features of the Antiphonary's preparation that provided all-important clues to the art of the Irish scriptorium. The freshness of this manuscript's black ink, impressions left by the dry-pointed stylus used to rule its folios,[24] pricking-marks serving as guides for the ruling of the vellum,[25] the coarseness of that vellum to the investigator's touch, the distinctive abbreviation signs on its pages,[26] these and its semi-uncial hand were traits shared by the Antiphonary with a family of Irish manuscripts and Northumbrian manuscripts composed under Irish influence.

Thanks in large part to the *terminus a quo* supplied by the Antiphonary, a new script could be announced—the Insular—possessing both Irish and Anglo-Saxon characteristics. In it we have proof that a cultural union had been effected between Britain and Ireland after 635, stronger than any hitherto known to exist. To Traube would go the honor of naming it the Insular hand. From Schiaparelli came approval of the name and a reminder that the Insular script was the inevitable consequence of geographical proximity and the binding force of Christianity.[27] Shortly, Lindsay and Cappelli offered new tests for identifying Insular manuscripts based on studies of the liberal use of abbreviations by Insular scribes, contrasted with their sparing use by Continental copyists.[28] Other paleographers showed the special importance of prick-marks serving as guides for textual lines in Insular manuscripts. When found in both margins, or on the outer bounding lines in both inner and outer margins, of books with non-Insular script, such prick-marks offer proof of Insular influence.[29]

By means of sustained investigation, other significant proper-
ties of Insular manuscripts have been established. It has been
found that Insular ink tends to retain its black freshness, whereas
the ink of Continental manuscripts has now a brownish hue.[30]
Also, Irish scribes and their Anglo-Saxon students ruled their
quires in a non-Continental manner. Instead of ruling before
folding, "Insular practice was to rule after the quire was formed,
usually on the recto pages; but if the impression on the verso
was faint, to rule that too."[31] Insular scriptoria did not invariably
follow Continental practice regarding the gatherings of their
books. Where the conventional quire in Continental manuscripts
is the quaternion, Insular scribes often show preference for the
quinion, a gathering of five bifolia, or ten leaves when folded.[32]
Insular scribes made use of punctuation far more than did their
Continental counterparts. Although a uniform system is lacking,
there is an Insular "preference for multiple points variously
grouped, now in a row, now in triangles, or otherwise."[33] Along
with a tendency toward profuse use of abbreviations in Insular
manuscripts, there has been noted also an ingenious use of
omission-signs, calling attention to a place in the text where an
omission has occurred in transcription. Continental omission-signs
*hd* (*hic deest*) and *hs* (*hoc supra* or *hoc scribus*) appear in many
Insular manuscripts as simply *h* or *d*. Insular scribes often placed
*d* in the text, answering it with *h* in the upper, lower, or lateral
margin.[34] In spelling, Insular scribes confuse *s* and *ss*, an error
seldom appearing in Continental manuscripts. Also, a striking
difference between Continental and Insular syllabification practice has been established with strange divisions such as *su-nt,
qu-od,* and *fo-ssam* not uncommon, the Irish being greater of-
fenders than the English here.[35]

And constantly before the eyes of anyone handling Insular
manuscripts produced either in England, Ireland, or the Continent is the semi-uncial hand with its tell-tale pointed descenders
(longer letters) and its ascenders (taller letters) widening into
wedge- or triangle-shaped tops.[36] Although this chief distin-
guishing mark of early Irish innovation with the semi-uncial remains intact in all Insular manuscripts, there are significant

differences to be seen between the books prepared by Irishmen and those executed by their Northumbrian students. The Irish scribe shows less dependence on rule and regulation and "behaves as if the written line were something elastic, not a fixed and determined space which has to be filled in a particular way. He seems often guided by whim and fancy. The English scribe, by comparison, is balanced and disciplined."[37] Working at home or in an English or Continental scriptorium, the Irish copyist often left other traces of his national temperament. A lack of uniformity in the make-up of gatherings, ruling either missing or not followed if present, a variety in the number of lines to a page, vellum that is rough to the touch and greasy, a page sprinkled with critical marks and abbreviations signify a manuscript that is probably the work of Irish rather than Northumbrian hands.[38]

Its secrets once yielded under the scrutiny of eyes sharper than those of the Cardinal's librarian, the Antiphonary assumed an honored place in the annals of paleography and the job of marshaling and interpreting the riddlesome facts of the Insular hand could proceed.[39] From its folios had come important dated evidence on the art of the scribe at Bangor, a monastery prominent in the account of cultural relations between Ireland and Britain given us in Adamnan's *Vita S. Columbae.*[40] Columba had conferred with Comgall of Bangor at Iona;[41] he had prayed for the safety of Comgall's monks "fighting against hostile powers in the air" in their curraghs on Belfast Lough;[42] he had said Mass for his visitors, Comgall and Brendan.[43] That a product of the Bangor scriptorium should contribute impressively to the piecing together of the achievement of Iona's missionaries to Northumbria is altogether fitting.[44]

Sous la coquille, il y avait un animal,
et sous le document, il y avait un homme.
Taine

*Chapter*
## V

## FOR GOD,
## COLUMBA, AND CUTHBERT

The four manuscripts to be discussed here are of genuine importance to a better understanding of the Irish contribution to Northumbria through Lindisfarne. Although their contents vary greatly, including as they do, a biography of Columba, a Psalter, and two Gospel texts, the manuscripts show interesting correspondences with each other. The biography and possibly the Psalter were done in the scriptorium at Iona; one of the Gospel texts may have been begun at Iona and completed in Ireland, and the second was executed at Lindisfarne. The saint's life and one of the Gospel texts are graced by the names of their makers. Three of the manuscripts have a close connection with St. Columba. All four documents show the Insular hand being refined and developed in the seventh and eighth centuries. All four are written in Latin, with the Gospel text prepared at Lindisfarne having invaluable Old English glosses. Fortunately, all four survived the ravages of time.

Of these four manuscripts, only one, a copy of the *Vita S. Columbae* known as the Schaffhausen Adamnan, enjoyed the colorless anonymity granted the Antiphonary of Bangor up to the time of its recognition by paleographers. Unlike the Psalter, or Cathach of Columba, no legend could attribute the hand-

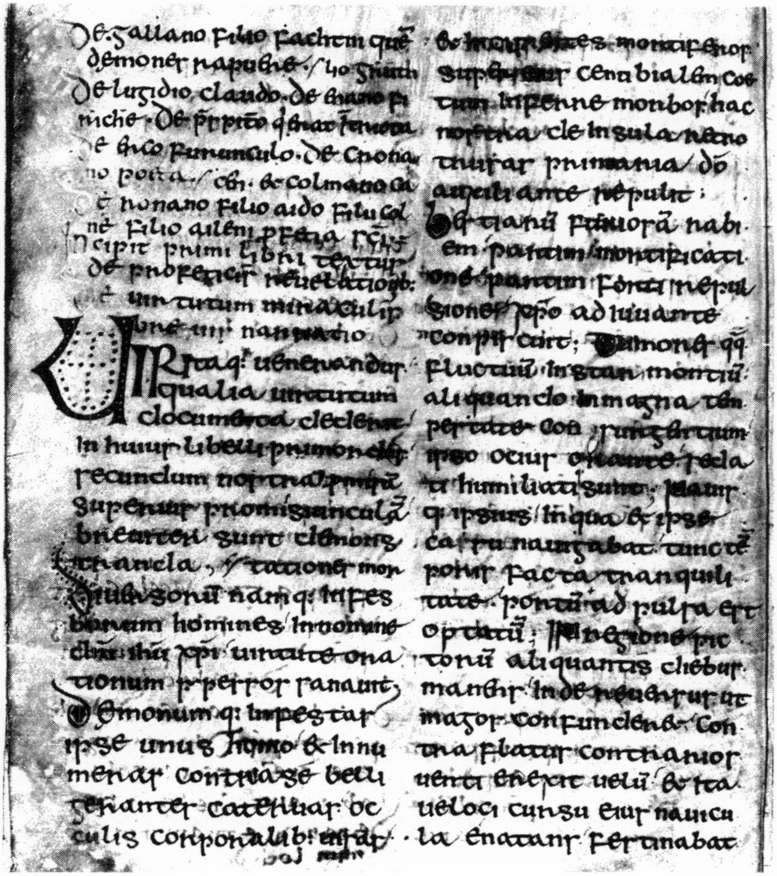

FIGURE 3—Schaffhausen Adamnan, folio 3v (Schaffhausen, Stadtbibliothek MS Gen. 1). Reproduced by courtesy of the Schaffhausen Stadtbibliothek, Switzerland.

writing of the Schaffhausen Adamnan to the saint himself. It boasted no gold-ornamented binding like that which greedy thieving hands wrenched from the Book of Kells, nor had it suffered the notoriety accorded the Book of Kells and the Lindisfarne Gospels for having survived inhumation and immersion.

Some time between Adamnan's death in 704 and his own in October, 713, Dorbene, scribe and prior at Iona, finished a transcription of the *Vita S. Columbae*. On its last page, his weary hand wrote these words: "I beseech those who wish to transcribe these books, yea, rather I adjure them by Christ, the Judge of the world, after they have diligently transcribed, carefully to compare and correct their copies with that from which they have copied them, and also to subjoin here this adjuration: 'Whoever readeth these books on the virtues of St. Columba, let him pray to the Lord for me Dorbbene, that after death I may possess eternal life.' "[1] From this point on, the history of the Schaffhausen Adamnan parallels that of the Antiphonary of Bangor to a remarkable degree. Like the Antiphonary, it became a refugee from the Viking raids, turning up at the Continental monastery of Reichenau where it remained until approximately 1795, to be acquired in that year for the town library at Schaffhausen, Switzerland.[2] Lying at the bottom of a book-chest with miscellaneous manuscripts bearing neither title nor number, it was re-discovered in 1845 by Frederick Keller.

An expatriate manuscript like the Antiphonary, the Schaffhausen Adamnan has dimensions approximating those of the Bangor manuscript, with sixty-eight leaves measuring nearly eleven by nine inches each and 138 pages with double columns of writing normally of twenty-eight lines each.[3] The script is "early and vigorous Irish minuscule mixed here and there with majuscule forms."[4] Further, Dorbene's ink mainly is that intense black used by the Bangor scribe.

The vellum of the Schaffhausen Adamnan was prepared to receive writing in the usual Irish way, the folios, rough and greasy in places, having been ruled on their recto sides with a drypointed stylus of wood or ivory. Carried to Northumbria, this scheme for ruling was installed in the scriptorium at Lindisfarne.

In his preparation of the Schaffhausen Adamnan Dorbene conformed with what is known to be Irish and Insular pricking practice.[5] Visible on both inner and outer margins of the manuscript are prick marks such as those seen in Figure 3.

In its forming of individual letters, Dorbene's hand is like that of the Bangor copyist. Specific resemblances between both scribes' execution of *u, t, n,* and *m* can be noted. Although displaying none of the versatility shown by the Bangor scribe in the treatment of the letter *a,* Dorbene lengthens *i* before *m* and *n* as did his contemporary. Both *o* and *e* of the diphthong *oe* are written separately, as in the Antiphonary.[6] Dorbene's abbreviations include the traditional Irish ones for *esse, non, nunc, prae, quae,* and *quoniam,* as well as others taught to Northumbrian students after 635.[7]

In copying what may have been Adamnan's own manuscript, Dorbene faithfully reproduced the tapered initials adorning it, a feature seen in Figure 3, line 13 of the first column, in the writing of "Vir Itaque." Irish scribal practice was to fringe initial letters with red dots; the Bangor scribe had followed this custom and so did Dorbene at Iona as may be seen in Figure 3, line 9 from the bottom of the left column. After fringing his initials, Dorbene filled in or daubed some with red or yellow pigment.[8] Spelling in Dorbene's manuscript is fair, with occasional odd interchanges of *a* for *e, e* for *a, i* for *a, ae* for *e,* and confusion of *b* and *p, e* and *i, f* and *ff, o* and *u,* and *s* and *ss.* Word division is often freakish.[9]

Despite its blemishes, however, the Schaffhausen Adamnan has a dignity befitting its age and its contents. Its script is regular and in one hand, and its coloring, although sparingly applied, is done with consistency. It has a "ceremonious or official character" that lends to it such prestige that one paleographer has suggested that it is an actual transcript of a signed copy by Adamnan.[10]

In contrast to the tone of circumspect reserve that marks the Schaffhausen Adamnan is the aura of speculation and mystery surrounding the psalmbook known as the Cathach of Columba, possibly Columba's personal Psalter.[11] The actions of the O'Donnell family, in whose custody the manuscript remained for cen-

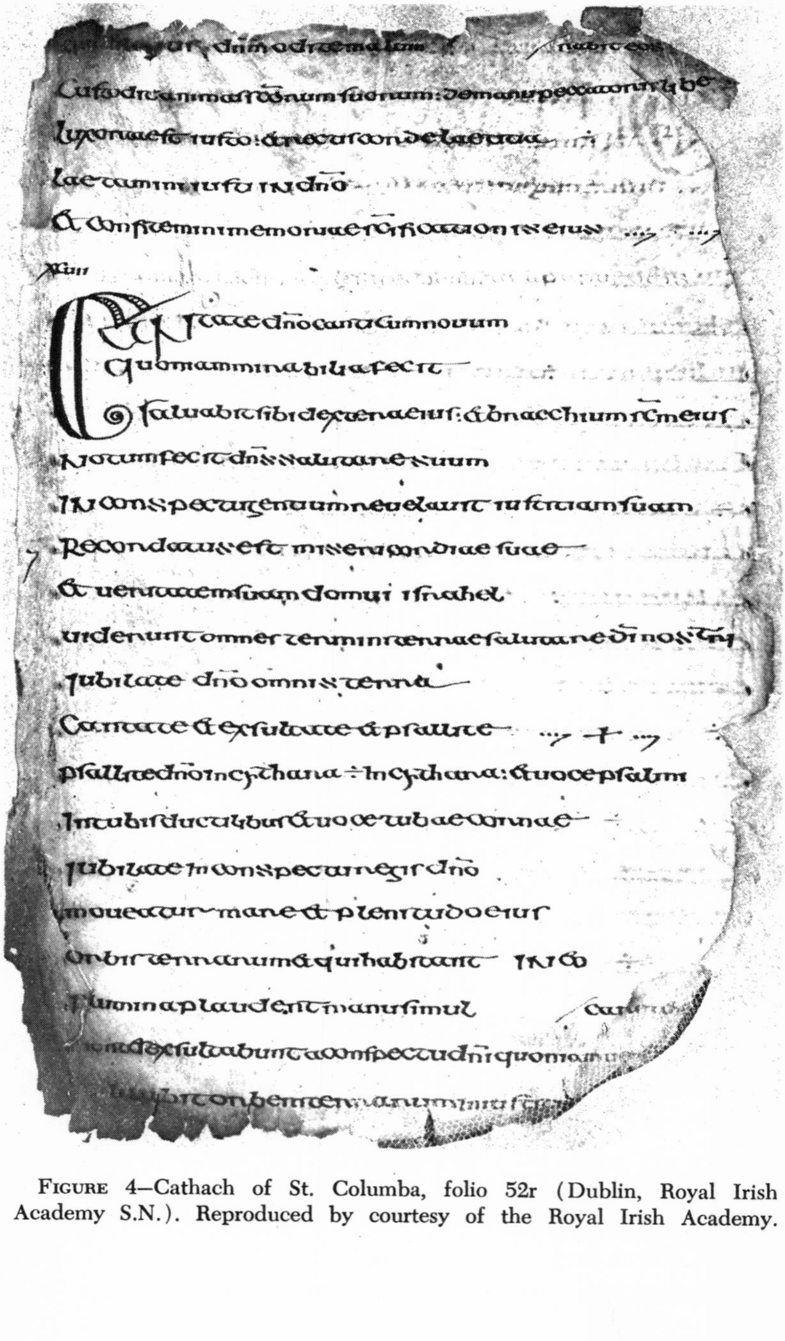

FIGURE 4—Cathach of St. Columba, folio 52r (Dublin, Royal Irish Academy S.N.). Reproduced by courtesy of the Royal Irish Academy.

turies, assured the maximum attention for the Cathach. Some time between 1062 and 1098 Cathbarr O'Donnell had it placed in a wooden case and in the fourteenth century a kinsman supplied it with a lid that defied opening by the curious. In 1732 when Daniel O'Donel carried it to France for safekeeping, its status as a relic deserving veneration was symbolized with its enclosure in a silver case. In 1802 the case was returned from a Paris monastery to Ireland, where Sir William Betham, an amateur antiquarian commissioned to trace the O'Donnell family line, was allowed to open it and inspect its contents. He wrote: "On one side was a thin piece of board covered with red leather, very like that with which eastern MSS are bound. It was so much injured by damp, as to appear almost a solid mass; by steeping it in cold water I was enabled to separate the membranes from each other, and by pressing each separately between blotting paper, and frequently renewing the operation, at length succeeded in restoring, what was not actually decayed, to a legible state."[12]

Noting that its script was a "small, uniform, but rather hurried hand," O'Curry in 1861 helped promote the tradition that this was indeed Columba's own hand and that the Cathach was the very copy of the Psalter belonging to St. Finnian of Moville which Columba had made without permission.[13] Characteristically Insular like the Antiphonary and the Schaffhausen Adamnan, the Cathach hand is an early stage of Irish majuscule with most of its letters sturdy and squat, showing no high shafts, and with bold triangular tags of *b*, *d*, and *l*. The round of *d*, *g*, and *p* is broader than it is high; *c* is rather higher than most of the other shaftless letters, and *d* is often open, whereas *r* is broad so that a word like *terrores* occupies a good deal of space.

Measuring now five inches by eight inches, the Cathach once probably contained all the psalms. As it survives, it is made up of fifty-eight consecutive leaves, all more or less mutilated. Apparently the scribe's plan called for twenty-five lines to each folio, in single columns.

The Cathach scribe used a dry-pointed stylus of wood or ivory to draw guide-lines after folding, "the direct impression being on the first recto of each gathering," on the recto side of each folio.[14] Prickings to guide ruling appear in both right and left margins.[15] The vellum used for the Cathach is less rough to the touch than that prepared for the Antiphonary. Despite Betham's immersion of the manuscript its ink retains a dark brown or black color.[16]

Artistic work in the Cathach is of a simple type with large tapered capitals at the beginning of each psalm drawn in black or brownish ink and outlined in red-dotted fringe. Because of the manuscript's immersion, initials originally colored with red and yellow pigment like those of the Schaffhausen Adamnan have nearly disappeared. As in the Antiphonary and the Schaffhausen Adamnan, *i* is lengthened before *n* and *m*, and *o* and *e* in the diphthong *oe* are written separately. Abbreviations are plentiful and of the Irish type used at Bangor and Iona.

The Cathach scribe was not as good a speller as Dorbene. He adds an *a,* as in "aegenum," or may omit the *a* as in "deargentate" and "terre." He substitutes *e* for *i,* as in "deluculo," "dimedio," and "redement." Substitutions of *i* for *e* occur, as in "cicidit," "dimissit," and "flagilla." Often found also is the substitution of *u* for *o,* as in "dulore," and "corroburavit." Frequently consonants are omitted or added freely. Examples of this blunder are "abysus," "confesio," "fluios," "gresus," "bassiliscum," "inlussionibus," "vissione," and "occassum."

Other scribal errors abound in the Cathach, caused perhaps not so much by the rapidity of transcription as the scribe's unsureness with Latin letters. Among 250 such mistakes are "veriae tuae" for "varietate," "in pinguine" for "et pinguedine," and "tribus" for "tribubus". The small number of corrections probably were made as the work progressed by a scribe who was an excellent penman, but one unable to transcribe both quickly and accurately.[17]

A careful study of the rubrics of the Cathach disclosed that they had been added by the same hand after completion of the text. It is possible that from these rubrics descended, ultimately, similar matter in certain seventh- and eighth-century Northumbrian texts including Codex Amiatinus, *De psalmorum libro exegesis* (attributed to Bede), and the Carlsruhe Psalter. One paleographer believes that these Northumbrian texts depend on a work which came from Ireland by way of Iona and paleographical evidence does much to support his belief.[18]

Our third manuscript, a Gospel text, has the utility of the Antiphonary, the dignity of the Schaffhausen Adamnan, the glamour of the Cathach of Columba, and artistic qualities peculiarly its own that have brought to it more popular and scholarly attention than any other Insular document. This is the Book of Kells, known as early as the eleventh century as *Soiscela mor Coluim Chille,* the "Great Gospel of Columcille."[19] Since 1661 it has rested in the library of Trinity College, Dublin, purchased in that year as part of the library of Gerald Plunkett. On November 18, 1539, Kells was surrendered to the Crown and it is likely that Richard Plunkett, its last abbot, kept the Book of Kells in his custody until turning it over to Gerald Plunkett.

Founded, according to tradition, by Columba, Kells became the sanctuary for the Iona monks forced to flee Viking violence and destruction after 804.[20] Since Kells was of little ecclesiastical importance before the arrival of survivors of the Iona *familia,* it has been suggested that the Book of Kells might actually have been written and ornamented in large part at Iona, and brought to Kells for completion. Such a theory would account for the unfinished illumination of the manuscript.[21]

In 1007, the chronicler charged with keeping the *Annals of Ulster* wrote of the narrow escape of the "chief relic of the western world," the "great Gospel of Colum-Cille . . . wickedly stolen in the night out of the western sacristy of the great stone-church at Cenannas [Kells]. . . . The same Gospel was found after twenty nights and two months, its gold having been taken off it and a sod over it."[22]

Of its 340 folios measuring nine and one-half by eight and one-half inches, only a few show discoloration caused by this earth burial. Each page of the Book of Kells has normally seventeen long lines on its surface with writing in a large round, or majuscule, semi-uncial hand. The ink used has the black color of manuscripts from Bangor and Iona. Ruling is done again on the recto side of the folios with the aid of a stylus. Pricking

argenteos · Aduenide que rebat oportunitatem ut eum traderet · Prima autem die azimorum accesserunt discipuli ad ihm dicentes ubi uis paremus tibi man ducare pascha At ihs dixit ite in ciuitatem ad quendam & dicite ei magister dicit tempus meum prope est Aput te facio pascha cum disci pulis meis · & fecerunt dis cipuli sicut praecepit illis ihs & parauerunt pascha Uespere autem facto discum bebat cum XII discipulis suis & edentib: illis dixit · Amen dico uobis quia unus uos

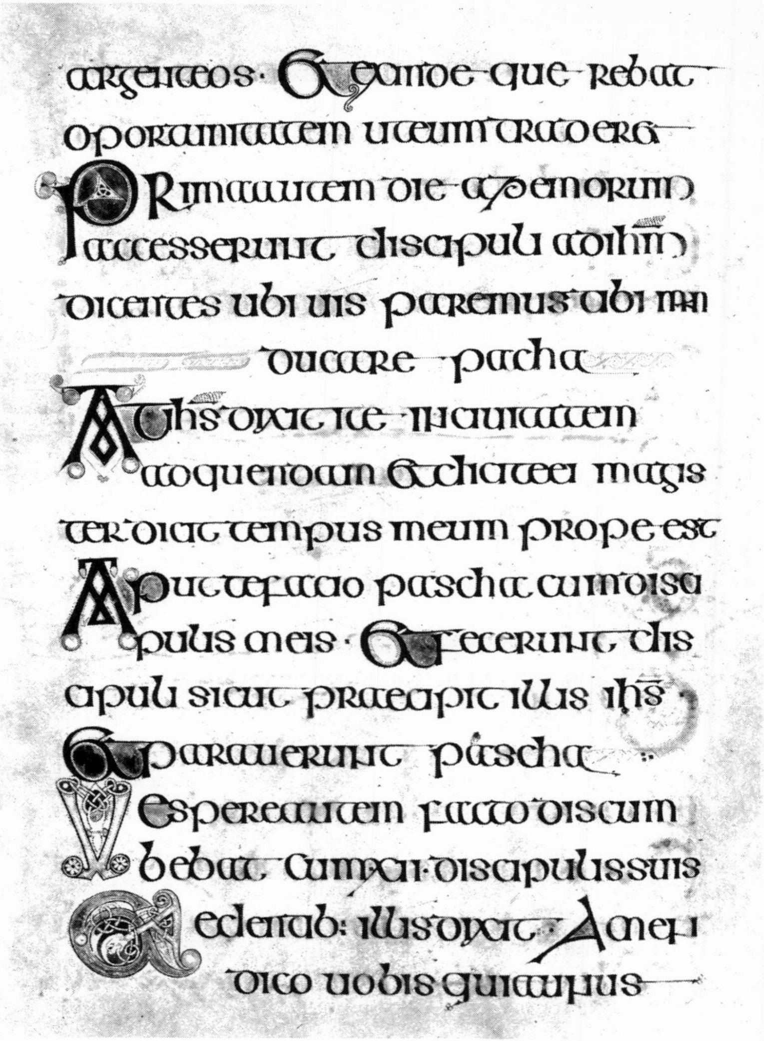

FIGURE 5—Book of Kells, folio 112v (Dublin, Trinity College 58[A.I.6]). Reproduced by courtesy of Trinity College.

marks to guide ruling are of the now-familiar Insular type, appearing on both inner and outer margins of each folio. Although the vellum is thick, its surface has been well prepared to receive both ink and pigments. Occasionally sheets have been stained purple with dye extracted from a variety of murex found on the shore of the Irish Channel.[23]

The fringed initials of the Antiphonary, the Schaffhausen Adamnan, and the Cathach of Columba are largely replaced in the Book of Kells by intricate designs created with rule and compass,[24] to which soft colors have been applied. Every folio has color or ornament on its surface whether initials or full-page decorations of Canon Tables and pictures of the evangelists. That limitless time was available to the makers of the Book of Kells is obvious from the precision of its draftsmanship and the painstaking care given to the application of pigment. Even small letters and groups of letters have color fillings.[25]

The same care was exercised to prevent scribal blunders of the type seen in the Cathach of Columba. Generous space is allowed between the lines of script and there is little economizing of the type seen in the Cathach, where words are crowded into a line and abbreviations are used to excess. Obviously the Book of Kells was not meant for exhibition to awe-struck converts by traveling missionary monks; rather its stateliness recommended its enshrinement in the church of the monastery's founder where it would be seen and remembered by countless pilgrims—lay and ecclesiastic. There is no paleographical evidence to rule out Iona and its founder Columba as the home and inspiration for the Book of Kells.

Inevitably, any consideration of the Book of Kells provokes comparison of it with a similar sumptuous codex, the Lindisfarne Gospels.[26] According to its famous colophon: "Eadfrith, bishop of the church of Lindisfarne, first wrote this book for God and St. Cuthbert and all the saints in general who are in the island. And Ethiluald, bishop of the people of Lindisfarne, bound and covered it on the outside, as he well knew how to do. And Billfrith, the hermit, worked the ornaments of metal that are on it outside. . . . And Aldred, an unworthy and very wretched priest, with God's help and St. Cuthbert's, glossed it in English. . . . Eadfrith, Oethiluald, Billfrith, Aldred made this gospel book for God and Cuthbert, and adorned it."[27] Eadfrith was Lindisfarne's bishop from 698 to 721, and it was to him that Bede dedicated his biography of St. Cuthbert. Ethilwald was bishop of Lindisfarne from 724 to 740. Of Billfrith, the artisan who fashioned the cover for the manuscript, nothing is known. Aldred, the "wretched priest," is remembered as the tenth-century writer of the Old English glosses of the manuscript.[28]

Unless we doubt the evidence of the colophon, we can assume that the manuscript was prepared at Lindisfarne *circa* 700, remaining there until 875, when it was moved, along with St. Cuthbert's body and certain relics of Oswald and Aidan, in the face of the mounting Viking terror. Tradition has it that at the very outset of the Lindisfarne monks' proposed journey to Ireland with their relics the Lindisfarne Gospels was accidentally dropped into the water of Solway Firth to be recovered unharmed. Other than this, nothing marred its progress through Northumbria and Durham in the company of saints' bones. Not until the eleventh century was it returned to Lindisfarne, after which all trace of the manuscript vanishes until its appearance as part of the library purchased by Sir Robert Cotton from Robert Bowyer, Keeper of Records in the Tower and Clerk of the Parliaments under James I. After joining the Cottonian collection, the codex shared a narrow escape with the *Beowulf* manuscript in the fire of 1731, but survived unscorched. Rebound in 1853 in its present jewelled and metal cover, it remains at the British Museum.

The manuscript of the Gospels of Lindisfarne consists of 258 folios, approximately 100 folios fewer than the Book of Kells in its original form. Although the writing is generously spaced, as in the Book of Kells, here there are two columns with twenty-four lines to a page instead of the seventeen lines of the Irish codex. The Lindisfarne scribe writes in Anglo-Saxon majuscule similar to the Irish semi-uncial hand seen in the Book of Kells, but conserves vellum by writing a smaller script.[29]

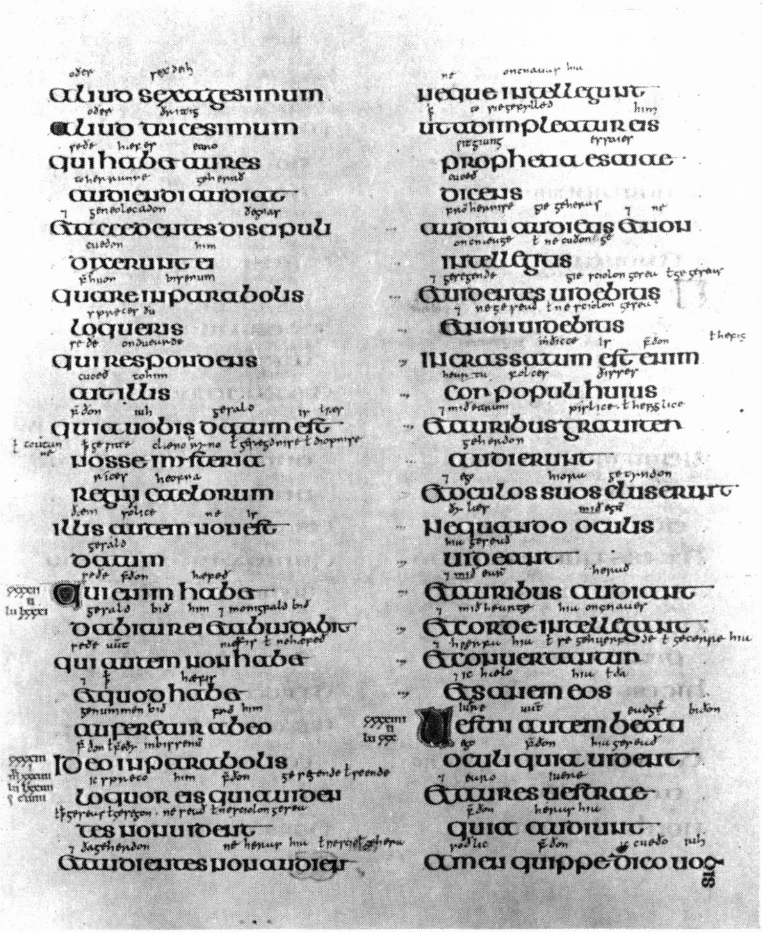

FIGURE 6—Lindisfarne Gospels, folio 52r (London, Cotton Nero D.iv). Reproduced by courtesy of the Trustees of the British Museum.

Eadfrith followed Insular ruling practice, his recto sheets receiving ruled lines that show through faintly on the verso sides. Prick-marks to guide the ruling appear on both inner and outer margins of the folios. Eadfrith chose the finest vellum for his book, ivory-white, smooth, well-polished, and perhaps even more uniform than that used by the makers of the Book of Kells. Standing out against the whiteness of the vellum is the rich black ink that helps distinguish Insular manuscripts from those of Continental scriptoria.[30]

Bishop Eadfrith did not allot as much time and care to the construction of capitals as had the scribe of the Book of Kells, whose capitals extend up to four lines high, averaging three lines taller than those in the Northumbrian codex.[31] Whereas the Irish scribe applied color profusely even on the ordinary pages of the text, Eadfrith used color sparingly on the equivalent pages of the Lindisfarne Gospels.[32]

Like the Irish Gospel text, the Lindisfarne codex contains four portraits of the evangelists, but sixteen pages of arcades enclosing Canon Tables as against ten in the Book of Kells.[33] The four full-page portraits of the evangelists are thoroughly Byzantine in design. Drawn in profile with cushion, desk, and footstool, the seated scribes are probably copied from portraits in Greek Gospels.[34] This Byzantine feature in the portrait pages of the Lindisfarne manuscript, its remarkably pure Vulgate text, and the South Italian origin of the list of feasts prefixed to the Gospels have prompted some doubt about Eadfrith's use of an Irish exemplar for any part of the manuscript. A logical explanation, however, can be offered for the presence of both Irish and Italian traits in its folios. Whereas the script and quite probably the ornament are of Irish origin,[35] Eadfrith wisely chose a Vulgate text less corrupt than the conventional Irish version, possibly taking it from one of the volumes brought back from Rome by Benedict Biscop before 674. He may have selected the Byzantine pictures of the evangelists from a Neapolitan *evangeliarium* brought to Lindisfarne by Abbot Hadrian of Naples who visited there with Archbishop Theodore near the time of Eadfrith's rule.[36] If so, Eadfrith showed good taste, for portraits in Italian

codices were unquestionably superior to those produced in Insular scriptoria.[37]

Eadfrith's codex joins the other manuscripts that have passed
briefly before us here in being Insular, but not provincial. The
Lindisfarne Gospels show that by 700 an inevitable cultural
syncretism was under way in a major Northumbrian scriptorium.
At least one scribe of the post-Whitby period planned and executed a major Gospel text, making discriminating aesthetic
choices from among Irish and Roman documents around him. It
was to Aidan's mission of 635 that Eadfrith ultimately owed his
skill in forming letters of the Word in ornate round Insular
majuscule. His knowledge of the polishing, folding, ruling, and
pricking of vellum was also part of the Iona bequest; so also
was his deftness in the drawing of capitals and in the application of pigment. For Eadfrith, and his fellow copyists in eighth-
century Insular scriptoria, racial antipathy, and the ostracism
and snobbery of ecclesiastical administrators that might conceal
or obscure this Irish heritage was an alien thing.

The Schaffhausen Adamnan and the Cathach, useful chiefly
in school and scriptorium, must share the fame accorded Gospel
codices like the Book of Kells, designed to impress the oldest
member of the *familia* as well as the newest convert. Meanwhile within earshot of the Lindisfarne scribes, mallets and
chisels in the hands of stone carvers were duplicating the utility,
adaptability, and magnificence of the Insular manuscripts on the
faces of great standing crosses.

Ar écnairc a chroichesium
as uaisliu cech croich . . .

(For the sake of his cross,
nobler than all crosses . . . )
From a poem attributed to St. Columba

*Chapter*
# V I

## ON THE MYSTERY
## OF THE CROSSES

Along with its traditional burden of Columba's dust, of Irish,
Scottish, and Norse royal bones, and of adventurers' coin-hoards,
Iona boasted stone crosses, the most famous being the fourteen-
foot high St. Martin's Cross that loomed above James Boswell as
he knelt before it to pray to Columba.[1] If we choose to believe
an anonymous writer of 1693, St. Martin's Cross shared the
monastery grounds with 359 others! In Adamnan's biography
of Columba, only two crosses are accounted for, one set before
the door of Iona's kiln to mark the fulfillment of Columba's
prophecy regarding the death of his uncle, and the second fixed
into a millstone at roadside to mark a spot where the saint
paused to rest near the end of his days.[2] Northumbrian visitors,
Oswald and Aldfrith among them, had seen these crosses and
been told of the effectiveness of Columba's "saving-sign."[3]
Whether raised to fix monastic boundaries, to commemorate the
founder of a particular church, or to sanctify former heathen
ground with the most potent Christian symbol, free-standing
high stone crosses like those at Iona, form a significant, yet puz-
zling part of the Irish cultural substratum in Lindisfarne's sphere
of influence.[4] Keeping in mind the results of our assay of this

substratum up to this point, let us check certain findings offered by scholar-detectives of art history, prepared to make plausible inferences and relationships.

Although the idea of the tall stone cross as a fitting monument came to Northumbria from the Celts,[5] disagreement exists as to whether the motifs on the faces of the Northumbrian crosses came from Continental or Irish sources. Strzygowski observes: "In all the excellent books on the subject of early Christian art in Ireland, Scotland, and England . . . the student invariably finds the same uncertainty in the critical appreciation of an art, which cannot be brought into connexion with Rome or explained in the usual way by reference to Roman monuments."[6] In the case of the stone crosses, this reluctance to admit the possibility of non-Roman influence is shown by Masai who is ready to see the Council of Whitby as terminating Irish cultural traditions in Northumbria.[7] Actually, there is growing evidence to indicate that Lindisfarne "remained Irish in spirit for much longer than one would expect and its art for a long time did not yield to English fashions."[8] Nevertheless, that portion of Masai's well-ordered argument that maintains English teachers came to Ireland to teach the Irish new methods of ornamentation and illumination deserves more attention than it has received. To Baldwin Brown "artistic elements which come in from outside and modify the native Anglian style are never direct importations from Irish sources, but are brought in by Scandinavians, whose receptivity to Irish influences . . . [was] phenomenal."[9] Another student of the problem of the direction of transmission claims that the Irish came to Northumbria "without any form of Celtic art-expression and left it capable of producing the highest forms of Irish Christian art."[10] He further deduces that members of the Northumbrian *familiae* who carved stone crosses were trained by Italian teachers, whereas the scribes and illuminators were trained by Irish masters. Events at Whitby expedited this phenomenon: "The continual communication between the early church of Northumbria and Ireland, either directly or via Iona, rapidly transmitted this new-found art to that country, and its growth was no doubt greatly furthered by the return home of many of the Irish ecclesiastics after their defeat at the Council of Whitby in 664."[11]

To the art historian is left the unhappy responsibility for settling finally the question of the chronology and the routing of several ornamental motifs appearing on the faces of crosses and on manuscript folios. At least one of these motifs, the spiral, is of Continental Celtic origin developed further by the Irish.[12] It appears on articles dating from the Bronze Age and is seen in pins and brooches of the sixth century executed in Wales and Saxon areas as a result of earlier visits to Ireland by British craftsmen. Certain folios of the Gospels of Lindisfarne and the Book of Kells display the spiral to good advantage.[13] In contrast, a second popular Insular motif, the interlace pattern, appearing on crosses carved at Lindisfarne, is not peculiarly Irish, but a synthesis of North Germanic and Eastern elements that can be followed back through Roman pavements and Greek vases to ancient Mesopotamia (Fig. 7).[14] In general, interlace sets a vermiform band, or a number of such bands, over the surface to be decorated. When the band in its course meets with another band, or another section of the same band, it intersects it, passing over and under alternately, after the manner of basketwork.[15] Like the spiral, interlace with Irish refinements assumes many intricate shapes, including plaits and knots, used alone or together on crosses, monuments, metal objects, and Insular manuscript folios.[16] The key pattern was perhaps adapted from the Roman mosaic floor and pavement and can be seen in nearly all the Gospel manuscripts and in a large proportion of the sculptured monuments of Ireland, Scotland, and Wales.[17]

Two other Insular motifs, zoomorphic and leaf-and-vine, are not of Irish origin although they are used extensively in manuscript decoration. The first came to Ireland by way of northern Europe and the Gothic peoples established along the north coast of the Black Sea.[18] But not until the meeting of Scandinavian and Irish cultures in the ninth century did its use become widespread. Lavish use of the zoomorphic can be noticed on the border interlaces of the Book of Kells.[19] The classical plant orna-

FIGURE 7—Fragments of Crosses at Lindisfarne. From *The Sculptured
Stones of Scotland*, ed. Stuart, Vol. II, Pl. XXVI. *A*–Left, interlacement
(plaitwork); right, braid and key pattern. *B*–Interlacement (square
knot). *C*–Interlacement (plaitwork) and portion of key pattern. *D*–Interlacement (plaitwork). *E*–Interlacement (plaitwork). *F*–Key pattern. *G*–
Human figures and plaitwork. *H*–Interlacement and key pattern. *J*–Interlacement (plaitwork). *K*–Portion of key pattern and animal figures.

ment motif is almost entirely alien to Irish art and wherever it appears (as in the Book of Kells), it is likely to represent a borrowed combination of Greek foliage ornament and Syrian vine scheme.[20]

Clearly, the carvings like those seen on fragments of crosses at Lindisfarne (Fig. 7) cannot claim to offer the same clear reflection of original and sustained Irish influence as do the manuscript hands.[21] Nevertheless, it remains difficult to believe that the Irish monk's skill was one limited solely to manuscript preparation, or one that when turned to stone-carving did not extend beyond the elementary process of rough-hewing the slab and blocking out its panels. The fragments shown in Figure 7 probably are from memorial crosses erected over the tombs of honored ecclesiastical personages. Remaining standing at Lindisfarne until 793, the date of the first Viking raid, they were razed one by one in the successive Scandinavian onslaughts of the ninth century. Stone masons constructing new buildings in the tenth and eleventh centuries made use of these shattered artifacts.[22]

Shown in Figure 8 are fragments of crosses raised at Coldingham in Berwickshire and at Durham, famous as the repository for St. Cuthbert's body after its peregrinations had ceased. According to Bede (*H. E.* IV, 25), it was at Coldingham that an Irishman named Adamnan (not Columba's biographer) forecast the destruction of that monastery's "goodly and high buildings" by fire. Possibly the fragments seen in Figure 8 are relics of this disaster. Incised on the fragments is the interlace ornament known to the Coldingham artisans.

The seven-foot high sandstone Monk's Stone at Tynemouth seen in Figure 9 resembles the Bewcastle and Ruthwell crosses known to students of Old English literature. Although weather-ravaged, it still displays incised sculpture, running ornament springing from a central stem with animals in its branches, as well as interlacement in combination with animal figures. Because of the predominant Continental and classical foliage motif on its face, the Tynemouth stone cannot be dated much before 700. Its carvings do not seem to be set in raised panels with the

*A*

*B*

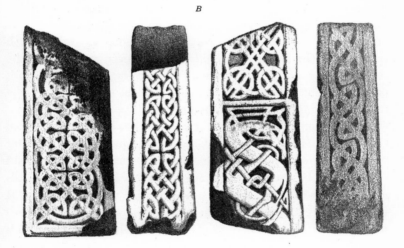

FIGURE 8—Fragments of Crosses at Coldingham and St. Oswald's, Durham. From *The Sculptured Stones of Scotland,* ed. Stuart, Vol. II, Pl. CX. *A*–Interlacement (plaitwork), Coldingham. *B*–Interlacement (plaitwork), St. Oswald's, Durham.

wide margins noticeable in the Bewcastle and Ruthwell Crosses. The panels on these crosses, and on the fragments from Lindisfarne, Coldingham, and Durham strongly resemble ornamented folios of manuscripts such as the Book of Kells and the Gospels of Lindisfarne. The absence of paneling on the Tynemouth stone, if not caused by weathering, may indicate that its carvers were not as much guided by the ornament of the manuscripts as were the Lindisfarne artisans.

At Ruthwell in Annandale, within eight miles of Dumfries, is the Ruthwell Cross. It stands over seventeen feet high with a sandstone shaft two feet wide and fifteen inches thick at its base, its faces sculptured and its sides covered with scroll-work.[23] On the broad faces appear figure-sculptures arranged in panels surrounded by flat borders with Latin inscriptions incised in block capitals (Fig. 10). Runic inscriptions on the narrow faces of the cross were found to be a portion of the Old English poem, *The Dream of the Rood*.[24] The figured subjects of the Ruthwell Cross all relate to the life and miracles of Christ with one important exception—one panel depicts a meeting of the desert fathers, Paul and Anthony (Fig. 10).[25]

Standing ten miles south of the Scottish border at Bewcastle in Cumberland is the Bewcastle Cross, raised inside the perimeter of a Roman fort six miles north of the Roman wall.[26] The head of this cross has been broken away from the shaft and it stands now over fourteen feet high, tapered from almost two feet at its base to slightly over a foot at its tip. Sunk about eleven inches into a massive base and fixed in its socket by lead is its sandstone shaft estimated to weigh five tons. The principal face of the Bewcastle Cross is turned toward the west. On its north and south faces are panels of interlace that resemble panels found in the Gospels of Lindisfarne.

After studying its decoration and lettering Brown seemed to accept a date of *circa* 675 for the Ruthwell Cross, one far too early when we recall that *The Dream of the Rood* itself, from which the cross inscription was taken, is not earlier than the eighth century.[27] Moreover, Brown's thesis that the Ruthwell Cross was an "imposing monument of Anglian Christianity" cre-

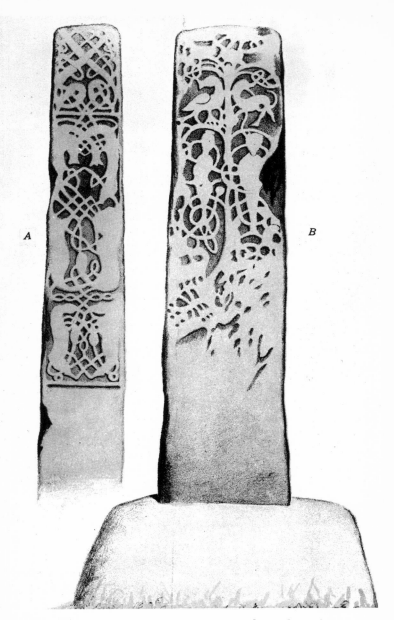

FIGURE 9—Monk's Stone at Tynemouth. From *The Sculptured Stones of Scotland*, ed. Stuart, Vol. II, Pl. LXXXIV. *A*–Animal figures and interlacement. *B*–Leaf-and-vine motif with animal figures.

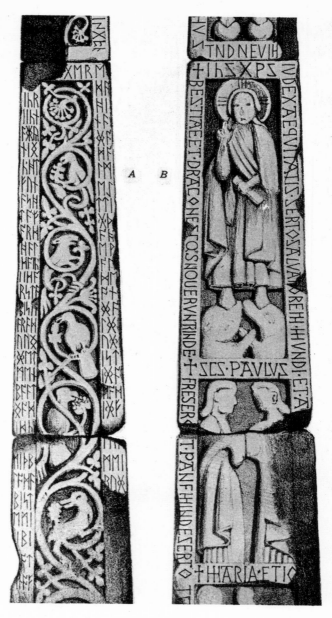

FIGURE 10—Panels from Ruthwell Cross. From *The Sculptured Stones of Scotland,* ed. Stuart, Vol. II, Pls. XIX, XX. *A*–Birds and beasts interlacement. *B*–Christ standing on the beasts (top); Paul and Anthony in the desert (bottom).

ated after the victory at Whitby seems illogical.[28] Is it likely that the limited victory at Whitby would be celebrated by raising a stone cross far from the scene of that victory and long after it had taken place? Brown affirms that the Bewcastle Cross was erected by the surviving retainers of Alcfrith (d. *circa* 670), a son of King Oswy present at the council, to mark his grave and commemorate his part in the censuring of the Irish. Since the Bewcastle inscription contains Alcfrith's name, a date close to 670–75 is probable.[29]

Brown did not realize that the figure-sculptures of the Ruthwell Cross are in the Celtic tradition rather than the Roman. The arrangement of these figures does not point up the Crucifixion (found on the lowest panel on the back of the cross), but rather the figure of Christ standing on the heads of two beasts.[30] Above him is John the Baptist holding the lamb of God and below are the desert fathers, Paul and Anthony, sharing a loaf of bread brought by the raven. The motif of Christ standing on the beasts, symbolizing his power over evil, suggests at first sight the imagery of heroic combat and the victories of heroes such as Beowulf over monsters such as Grendel.[31] Only recently has there been pointed out the possibility of a close affinity between the feats of Irish saints in overcoming monsters, the deeds of their hero counterparts in epic literature, and the exploits of Beowulf himself.[32]

According to the Ruthwell Cross inscription, "Jesus Christ: the judge of righteousness: the beasts and dragons recognized in the desert the savior of the world." The beasts have been humbled. Their postures indicate obeisance to a master. The figures of John and the desert fathers fit easily into context with the beasts. To Irish *peregrini* John stood as a prototype of Christian asceticism, who set an example for survival in the wilderness.[33] Paul and Anthony became figures of cultish admiration for Irish hermit and anchorite monks in the eighth and ninth centuries, and both are frequently represented on the crosses of the ninth and tenth centuries. In the early ninth-century Stowe Missal their names appear immediately after those of the martyrs.[34] In Irish hagiographical tradition saints and their converts exer-

cised miraculous powers over the fauna with whom they shared
wild, remote, and desolate areas.[35] The figure of Christ standing
on the beasts as given us by the Ruthwell sculptor is definitely
in this tradition.

In contrast to the Ruthwell Cross, both Paul and Anthony
are omitted from the Bewcastle Cross, and depicted there is not
the Christ of the desert, but a militant, conquering Christ in
the Roman tradition. Schapiro's hypothesis is that the Ruthwell
Cross stands as evidence of the presence in the second half of
the seventh century of a community of Britons and Anglian settlers ruled by Northumbrians whose loyalty to the Irish brand
of Christianity lasted long after 664.[36]

The fragments of *The Dream of the Rood,* sometimes attributed to Cynewulf[37] and found on the Ruthwell Cross, provoke
speculation as to the link between the first English poet to sign
his name and Irish elements in the eighth-century Northumbrian
cultural milieu represented on the faces of the stone cross at
Dumfries. In the famous autobiographical passage of the *Elene*
(ll. 1236 ff.)[38] Cynewulf tells of studying the lore of the Cross
(*sigebeacne*) in various books and writings (*bocum . . . gewri-
tum*).[39] Undoubtedly one source that he consulted carefully was
Adamnan's transcribed account of the sacred places of Christianity, *De locis sanctis.* This document very likely supplied
impetus to the erection of stone crosses and literature venerating
the Cross. In it, Adamnan tells how the Gaulish Bishop Arculf
saw at Jerusalem a "great cross of silver, fixed in the same spot
where once stood fixed the wooden Cross on which suffered the
Saviour of the human race."[40] At another point in the narrative
Arculf tells of having seen the sponge that had been soaked in
vinegar and the "spear of the soldier with which he smote
through the side of the Lord as He hung on the Cross."[41] Cynewulf and the avid readers preceding him read also of a "lofty
column, standing in the middle of the city [Jerusalem] . . .
set up on that spot where a dead young man came to life
again when the Cross of the Lord was placed on him. . . . "[42]

Arculf's narrative transcribed at Iona goes on to a colorful
description of the site of Christ's baptism by John where the

pilgrim may look on a wooden cross set in the river.[43] Chapter III of Adamnan's version of Arculf's tour gives a detailed description of the shrine of shrines at Constantinople, calculated to impress deeply both Irish and Northumbrian clerics. Adamnan writes: "In the northern part of the interior of the house is shown a very large and very beautiful ambry, in which is kept a wooden chest, which is similarly covered over with wooden work: in which is shut up that wooden Cross of Salvation on which our Saviour hung for the salvation of the human race."[44] Adamnan describes the kissing of the Cross carried out on appointed days by the Emperor and the highest clergy, and he goes on to tell that "there are not two but three short pieces of wood in the Cross, that is, the cross-beam, and the long one which is cut and divided into two equal parts."[45]

Cynewulf, the poet, and Cynewulf, Bishop of Lindisfarne ( d. *circa* 782), are not one and the same.[46] Neither is the poet the author of *The Dream of the Rood.* However, it is almost certain that Iona's influence on the poetic imagination was spurred by contact with Adamnan's widely-circulated *De locis sanctis.*[47] And although Iona must share credit with the Continent for the ornament on crosses at Lindisfarne, its influence shows forth in the Irish-inspired motif of the desert fathers on the Ruthwell panel and in those stirring passages of the *Christ* in the Exeter Book where Cynewulf exalts the cross.[48]

Over the heather the west wind blows,
I've lice in my tunic and a cold in my nose.

. . . . . . . . .

The mist creeps over the hard grey stone,
My girl's in Tungria; I sleep alone.
From "Roman Wall Blues," W. H. Auden

*Chapter*
# V I I

## THE
## CELTO-SAXON
## ELEGY

In its learning, its manuscripts, and its stone crosses, Northumbrian culture exhibited adaptability and ease of assimilation with Celtic and Continental elements. Now we shall see evidence of how the Anglo-Saxon poets fashioned an elegiac tradition somewhat independent of Continental literary forms. In doing so they were taking stock of their past by drawing in part on a store of annals, chronicles, saints' lives, and popular literature that reflects sustained contact with Celtic monasticism.

When Leofric the first bishop of Exeter died in 1072, over four hundred winters had passed since Aidan's arrival at Bamburgh, and the sun had set more than one hundred thousand times since that first fateful Viking carnage at Lindisfarne. With one act before his death, Leofric helped preserve important evidence of the Saxon debt owed to scriptoria at Lindisfarne and other northern monasteries where the Irish hand had been taught. To his church he had donated an item described as "•i• micel englisc boc be gehwilcum þingum on leoðwisam geworht" ("one great English book on all manners of subjects wrought in verse"). Estimates vary slightly as to the age of this manuscript called the Exeter Book, but Flower's date for its composition—some time between 970 and 990—seems reasonable. The product of a southern scriptorium where scribal techniques originally introduced at Lindisfarne survived, the Exeter Book exhibits the familiar Insular minuscule with pointed descenders and flat-topped triangles (see Fig. 11).[1] Its ink retains Insular blackness; folio ruling has been done with stylus on both recto and verso sides, and prick marks to guide ruling are visible on nearly all folios of the manuscript.[2] On one folio appears a traditionally Irish type of scribal signature.[3]

It is not its script alone, however, that reminds us of the Iona heritage of the Exeter Book. Indeed there are tenth-century manuscript hands which look much more Irish than the hand of the Exeter Book. It is in two of the elgiac poems of the Exeter Book that there appears evidence of the influence of Irish monastic culture on the world of the Old English poet.[4]

It has been difficult for literary detectives to concede that poems like the Old English *Ruin* and *Wife's Lament* apparently owe little to Greek elegy of the type appearing alongside Greek lyric poetry from the eighth to the fifth centuries B.C. Nor does there seem to be any English debt to Roman elegy— the *elogia* or *monumenta privata* that glorified special persons, and the *laudationes* or *orationes funebres*. Both were formal laudations in honor of departed family members.[5] Cicero mentions *laudes* in *De inventione* (II, 59),[6] and Quintilian refers to *funebres* in *Institutio oratoria* (XI, 3),[7] but there is no evidence that this form of Roman elegy was known to Germanic tribes in the first century after Christ. Writing in A.D. 98, Tacitus (*Germania*, 27) tells only that the Germanic funeral was not typified by any pretentious death song and lament at the bier of the hero.[8] A definition of *lamentatio* given in an extract from the life of King Offa of Mercia (d. 796) is offered by Du Cange to illustrate how the Germanic funeral rite could incorporate elements of Christian burial, but there is no evidence that such a ceremony acted as the forerunner for the elegiac note found in the poems of the Exeter Book.[9]

As first detected by English scholar-antiquarians, the elegiac note in Old English poetry seemed vague and amorphous in that

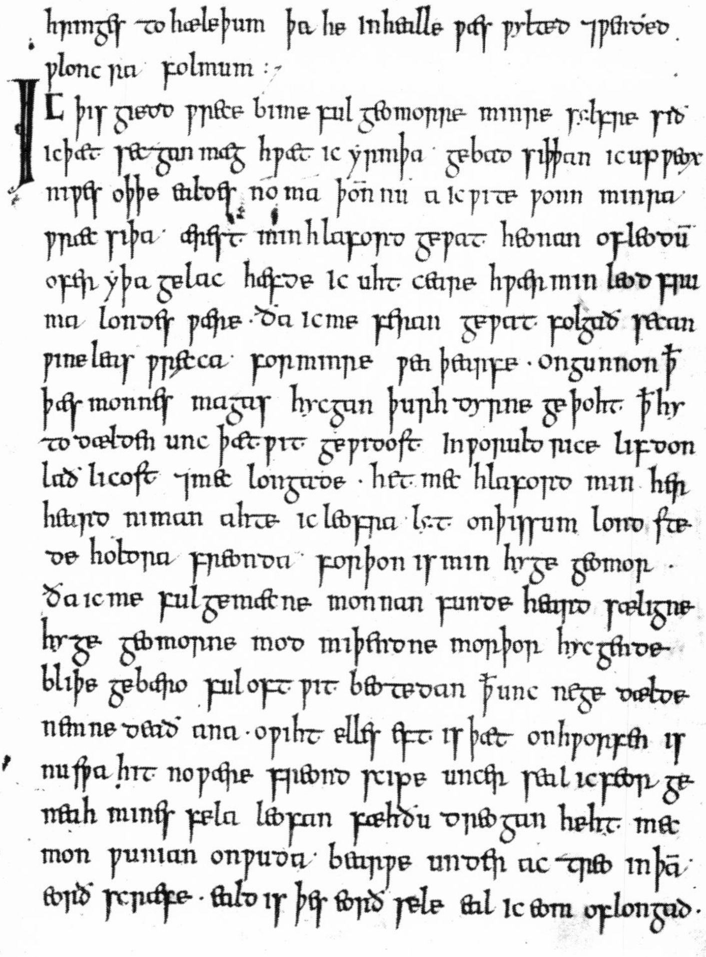

hringest to hæleþum þa he inhealle wæs wylted 7 wsnioed.
wlonc wa wolmum :-
IC þis giedd wrece bi me ful geomorre minre sylfre sið
ic þæt secgan mæg hwæt ic yrmþa gebad siþþan ic up weox
niwes oþþe ealdes no ma þonne nu a ic wite wonn minra
wræcsiþa ærest min hlaford gewat heonan of leodum
ofer yþa gelac hæfde ic uht ceare hwær min leodfru
ma londes wære ða ic me feran gewat folgað secan
wineleas wræcca for minre weaþearfe ongunnon þæt
þæs monnes magas hycgan þurh dyrne geþoht þæt hy
todælden unc þæt wit gewidost in woruldrice lifdon
laðlicost 7 mec longade het mec hlaford min her
heard niman ahte ic leofra lyt on þissum londste
de holdra freonda forþon is min hyge geomor
ða ic me ful gemæcne monnan funde heardsæligne
hyge geomorne mod miþendne morþor hycgende
bliþe gebæro ful oft wit beotedan þæt unc ne gedælde
nemne deað ana owiht elles eft is þæt onhworfen is
nu swa hit no wære freondscipe uncer sceal ic feor ge
neah mines felaleofan fæhðu dreogan heht mec
mon wunian on wuda bearwe under actreo in þam
eorðscræfe eald is þes eorðsele eal ic eom oflongad.

FIGURE 11—Exeter Book, folio 115a (Exeter Cathedral Library). Reproduced by courtesy of the Dean and Chapter of Exeter.

it did not conform with classical tradition by directing itself to the praise of any specific person. Bishop Percy declared poems like *Widsith, Deor,* and the *Seafarer* had been composed by Anglo-Saxon minstrels and harpers whose talents were chiefly calculated to entertain and divert.[10] In the preface to his *History of English Poetry* Warton stated "our Saxon poems are for the most part little more than religious rhapsodies."[11]

First to sense the distinctive character of the Old English elegies was Conybeare, who wrote of the *Wife's Lament*: "His situation and feelings are expressed with more pathos, and his lonely retreat amidst the woods exhibits more power of description than can be usually found in Saxon poetry."[12] Of the *Ruin,* Conybeare confessed: "The editor was unwilling, however, to suppress a fragment of so much interest, and so superior, both in picturesque description and in the tone of moral feeling which pervades it, to the great mass of Saxon poetry."[13] To Isaac Disraeli, on the other hand, all Old English poetry, including the elegies, was the poetry of barbarism, a "collection of short hints rather than poetical conceptions, curt and ejaculative; [in which] a paucity of objects yields but a paucity of emotions, too vague for detail, too abrupt for deep passion, too poor in fancy to scatter the imagery of poesy."[14]

For over half a century German, French, and American scholars have probed the elegiac poems. Did the poems develop spontaneously from national literature, or from a foreign source grafted to the stem of national literature? Are they the product of long development, or did they spring suddenly from the genius of highly gifted poets? Should they be treated individually, or as a distinct group, well-known and widespread? Looking for counterparts to the Old English vernacular poems in Old Irish and Old Norse poetry, a German attracted to *Anglistik* found in the death laments of the *Egils saga* proof for his theory that the Germanic elegiac form developed independently from the epic. The cuckoo motif of the *Husband's Message* Sieper believed to have a Celtic source.[15]

A French scholar studying primarily the theme of nature in Old English poetry was among the first to take into account the influence of the Lindisfarne mission: "Ce sentiment de la nature est-il une survivance païenne ou un aspect de la pensée chrétienne ou encore un amalgame de ces deux éléments? Ces éléments sont-ils véritablement opposés; dans quelle mesure peut-on identifier chacun d'eux et les dissocier l'un de l'autre."[16] Believing that the love of nature appearing in Old English poetry was due to the influence of Irish Christianity in Northumbria, Pons wrote: "Bien que les moines irlandais, venus avec Columban, préférassent fonder leurs monastères en des lieux rocheux et sauvages comme Iona, Lindisfarne ou Whitby, les religieux anglais issus d'eux aimèrent à orner la solitude de leurs cloîtres de pelouses et de fleurs, à les entourer de jardins et de bosquets. . . . "[17] Along with a love for nature, the Irish missionaries at Lindisfarne gave their converts a feeling for the tragic side of life. It is these two themes, writes Pons, that "souvent alternent en contrastant, se soutiennent l'un l'autre, s'enrichessent mutuellement."[18]

Recent scholarship on the elegiac poems of the Exeter Book has offered intensive analysis of individual poems rather than generalizations applicable to all the poems.[19] In several such studies of the *Seafarer*, the possible influence of Irish monasticism on the poet has been given new attention. In the *Seafarer* the poet depicts the tumultuous, icy winter seas in terms so vivid as to rival similar passages in *Beowulf* (ll. 210–24, 1130–33, 1903–13) or the *Elene* (ll. 237–46).[20] Yet man of the sea images could well have been constructed by a sharp-eyed landsman living by the sea, perhaps at Lindisfarne.[21] The poem may well give poetic expression to the *peregrinatio pro amore Dei* with which all Northumbrian converts after 635 were familiar.[22] Inevitably in discussing such poems as the *Ruin*, the *Seafarer*, and the *Wife's Lament*, once it is agreed that a line of direct descent from any Germanic poetic tradition is difficult to substantiate, it becomes necessary to look to the Celtic elements as a likely source for the elegiac lament, gnomic materials, and awareness of natural surroundings that make the Old English poems so noteworthy.[23] Let us do this first with the *Ruin*.[24]

More than two centuries lie between Gildas' gloomy jeremiad

and Alcuin's lament penned after the sack of Lindisfarne.[25] Gildas, the Romano-Briton, vented his grief at the collapse of a culture, and Alcuin, the Englishman, believed only a heart of stone could remain impervious to the destruction of Lindisfarne. Both are prime representatives of an elegiac tradition dating from the fourth and fifth centuries and strengthened under the influence of Irish culture in Northumbria.

Although Gildas' *De excidio et conquestu Britanniae* is the first document to substantiate the tradition of lament for vanishing and dilapidated monuments, British bishops of York, London, and probably Lincoln who attended the Council of Arles (314), as well as those who sat with the Councils of Sardica (347) and Ariminum (359), bore eye-witness reports of the decay of Roman culture in Britain to their fellow churchmen.[26] Ecclesiastical travelers through Britain in the fifth century, such as Palladius and Germanus, with their own eyes had seen crumbling Roman villas, temples, and tombs, along with occasional Christian-inscribed stones and altars.[27]

Perhaps himself an Anglo-Irish *peregrinus,* the poet of the *Ruin* knew at first or second hand of impressive ruins reflecting an architectural splendor in sharp contrast to the mud and wattle thatched huts in the vicinity of Bamburgh and Lindisfarne.[28] At Roman Chester stood ruins linking that city and a nearby Celtic monastery with an event momentous in Insular history, judging by the care with which English and Irish annalists memorialized it. This was the massacre of the *familia* at the Welsh monastery of Bangor Iscoed, or Bangor-on-the-Dee as it came to be known to later chroniclers. Events leading up to the woe befalling Bangor are reported by Bede (*H. E.* II, 2). At the time of Augustine's arrival in Kent (597) Bangor was a Celtic religious stronghold with "7 companies, with each company his several assigned ruler, none of these companies had less than 300 persons, who did all ever live by the labor of their own hands." Bangor Iscoed held out stubbornly against Augustine's attempts to bring it into the Roman camp, finally incurring a fateful prophecy from his lips to the effect that "if they would not have peace with brethren, they should have war from ene-

mies; and if they would not preach to the English nation the
way of life, they should through their hands suffer the vengeance
of death." Within a little more than a decade the Bangor con-
gregation suffered a calamity rivaling those of which Gildas had
wailed in *De excidio*. In 613 a Northumbrian army under Ethelfrith engaged a British host at Chester. Grouped together on
the sidelines, praying earnestly for a British victory, stood a
large number of the Bangor brethren. Seeing them, the wrathy
Ethelfrith ordered their slaughter.[29]

Chronicles kept by Insular ecclesiastics corroborate one another on the Chester massacre. The *Anglo-Saxon Chronicle* says
that "two hundred priests" were killed.[30] The *Annals of Clonmacnoise* tell of the battle of Chester, where "Folinn McConan,
king of the Brittans was killed by Ethalfrid, who haveing the
victory, Died himselfe instantly."[31] The *Annals of Tigernach* refer to the "Praelium Carleonense ubi Sancti occisi sunt. . . . "
Likewise the *Annals of Inisfallen* reveal "Cath Legeoin in quo
ceciderunt multitudines sanctorum."[32] In the *Annals of Ulster*
appears this entry: "The battle of Caer-legion, in which holy
men were slain, and Solon son of Conaen, King of the Britons,
fell."[33] The catastrophe is noted carefully in *Annales Cambriae*.[34] The phantom annalist of O'Rahilly's hypothetical "Ulster
Chronicle" also recorded the grim happenings at Chester using
a chronicle composed at Iona.[35] In Wales, in addition to the
*Annales Cambriae* entry, the ordeal of Bangor is reflected indirectly in lines of a bardic poem that gives the genealogy of
Northumbrian kings.[36]

At Iona and Lindisfarne the story of the martyrdom at Chester must have been told and retold. Many a *peregrinus* could
describe the site of Bangor, still marked by debris at the time
of William of Malmesbury (d. 1143), who described it as a
scene of rack and ruin.[37] The indefatigable sixteenth-century
traveler, John Leland, gives a lengthy description of the ruins
at Bangor, mentioning "foundations of squarid stonys, and Ro-
mayne money is founde there."[38] Thomas Pennant recalls Bangor as "the site of the most antient British monastery," and as
late as 1836 a Welsh antiquarian reported traces of extensive
buildings standing there.[39]

The poet of the *Ruin* is describing more than mere crumbling walls.[40] He offers concrete details that have encouraged attempts to identify the site as the Romano-British watering place of Bath.[41] Those concluding lines of the *Ruin* telling of hot flowing water have helped gain acceptance for the Bath identification:

> Stanhofu stodan, stream hate wearp
> widan wylme; weall eall befeng
> beorhtan bosme, þaer þa baþu waeron,
> hat on hreþre. . . .                                         (ll. 38–41)

> (There stood the courts of stone. Hotly within,
> The stream flowed with its mighty surge. The wall
> Surrounded all with its bright bosom; there
> The baths stood, hot within its heart. . . . )[42]

Clearly, the poet has a city of great size in mind:

> Wraetlic is þes wealstan, wyrde gebraecon;
> burgstede burston, brosnað enta geweorc.
> Hrofas sind gehrorene, hreorge torras,
> hrungeat berofen, hrim on lime,
> scearde scurbeorge scorene, gedrorene,
> aeldo undereotone.                                           (ll. 1–6)

> (Wondrously wrought and fair its wall of stone,
> Shattered by Fate! The castles rend asunder,
> The work of giants moldereth away,
> Its roofs are breaking and falling; its towers crumble
> In ruin. Plundered those walls with grated doors—
> Their mortar white with frost. Its battered ramparts
> Are shorn away and ruined, all undermined
> By eating age.)[43]

Chester, built and garrisoned by the Legio XX Valeria Victrix, meets the description better than Bath.[44] It is doubtful that a twenty-three acre watering place like Bath contained roofs, towers, the red wall, and high gate of the *Ruin*. Ruined Chester and the city described in the Old English poem have significant features in common that were still apparent in the twelfth century. Giraldus Cambrensis describes the home of the Twentieth Legion as a "city . . . of undoubted antiquity, and handsomely built of masonry, with courses of bricks, by the Romans. Many vestiges of its former splendour may yet be seen;

immense palaces, formerly ornamented with gilded roofs, in imitation of Roman magnificence, inasmuch as they were first raised by the Roman princes, and embellished with splendid buildings; a tower of prodigious size, remarkable hot baths, relics of temples . . . all inclosed within fine walls, parts of which remain standing."[45]

Chester's walls were built of the same red Bunter sandstone utilized by Christian stone-masons whose handiwork in the form of tombs and altars dotted the countryside.[46] More important, "The Bunter Sandstone is a noted water-bearing rock throughout Cheshire and South Lancashire. . . . Earthern [sic] pipes of Roman type have been discovered in excavations at various times, laid east and west towards Boughton. At this locality the sands and gravels underlying the Upper Boulder Clay are heavily charged with water which often overflows in springs. Such surface indications are readily seen and, according to Shrubsole (1893), probably formed the main water supply for Roman Chester."[47] The Old English poet of the *Ruin* might well have seen the red stone ruins of Chester, a site linked in Insular chronicles with the shameful act of Ethelfrith. He could have fashioned the lines pertaining to the hot baths after comprehending the significance of the surface springs, earthen pipes, and hypocausts.

For centuries English chroniclers were impressed by ancient Chester. In his *Polychronicon* Ranulf Higden (d. 1364), writes that Chester was "the chiefe cite of Northe Wales in the tyme of Britones. . . ."[48] Like Giraldus, he comments on the vastness of its ruins: "For hit scholde seme to a man beholdenge the fundacion of hit that werke to be rather of the labor of gigantes, other Romanes, then of Britones."[49] Higden's reference to Chester's destruction by "men of Northumberlande" under "kyng Elfride" recalls again the tie between the fate of the Bangor monks and the ruined city of Chester established by Insular writers.

In contrast, it is doubtful the ruins at Bath at any time presented the awesome sight described in the *Ruin*. Despite the label "queen of Romano-British cities" applied to it by a contemporary scholar, Bath was not a major fortress-city like Chester, nor even a medium-sized military outpost, but rather a recuperation oasis for Roman Britain. Archaeological evidence suggests that Bath quickly sank into oblivion, its few buildings dismantled by successive marauders. Even the hot spring waters forced their way upward with difficulty through the silt and debris which marked the site of Aquae Sulis and the Temple of Sul Minerva in the eighth century.[50]

Astride a probable route for settlers, raiding parties, and holy men from Ireland in the sixth century, as well as a host of ecclesiastical visitors bound from Northumbria to Ireland after 635, stood the ruins of Roman Chester. The elegiac poet, as a member of an Irish-Northumbrian community like Lindisfarne, would draw on sights at Chester, tactfully leaving out specific reference to Ethelfrith's misdeed. Thus the Old English poet worked in an Insular literary tradition instituted by Gildas, strengthened and encouraged by Irish contact,[51] and revived by Alcuin when he and other clerical writers sadly beheld Lindisfarne, the citadel of Insular culture, under attack by Germanic rivals from Scandinavia in 793.

Alongside the *Ruin* stands a second poem in the Exeter Book that seems to reflect the independence of Anglo-Saxon elegy from its classical counterpart, while underlining the lasting impact of Celtic monasticism on Northumbria in the post-Whitby era. This is the *Wife's Lament*.

Young Benedict of Nursia unwittingly threw himself into the spiritual breach as well as the brambles when rejecting the Tempter in the form of a beautiful female.[52] Benedict's act was opportune, for the Church was losing ground in its fight to maintain the celibacy advocated by Jerome, Ambrose, Augustine, and Hilary. Indeed, in 502, a new bishop of Arles wrote Pope Symmachus imploring that a precept forbidding marriage to nuns be issued,[53] despite the fact that as early as 325 the Council of Nicaea (attended by British bishops) had legislated against all but the most innocuous form of female companionship for monastic clergy.[54] Ecclesiastical legislators meeting at Nicaea were anxious to discourage the practice of the *subintro-*

*ductae* that would have its bothersome equivalents in the *foca-rista* and *focaria* of later times.[55] Oddly enough, there seems to be no evidence of official prohibition of an ascetic test which placed a beguiling female in the very cell of the celibate Irish monk. This practice, undoubtedly known to Northumbrian converts after 635, has gone almost unnoticed by scholars. Thirty years ago a French Celticist claimed this test of celibacy to be of minor importance in the Irish monasteries: "Voilà tout ce que les textes latins ou la littérature irlandaise nous apprennent sur les manifestations de syneisaktisme en Irlande. C'est donc évidemment exagérer que d'affirmer, comme l'a fait H. Achelis, que 'l'ancienne Eglise d'Irlande fit de cette forme d'ascétisme le pilier fondamental de son organisation.' Pas plus en Irlande que dans le reste de la chrétienté, l'autorité ecclésiastique n'a jamais recommandé ces périlleux rapprochements des sexes."[56] Although Gougaud reproaches Achelis for unseemly exaggeration, evidence from Insular sources shows that the female consort sometimes tested mightily the powers of abstinence in Irish ecclesiastics like those whose *vitae* were reviewed in our first chapter. From the *Hisperica Famina,* a document probably offering insights into the pattern of Gaulish Christianity introduced to Ireland in the fourth and fifth centuries, comes the poem called *The Ascetic Dismisses His Wife.* Described as a poem that "breathes the spirit of Celtic monasticism,"[57] it presents the touching parting of husband and wife necessitated by the former's wish to exchange the intimate companionship of a marriage partner for lonely dedicated service to a spiritual master. The husband's rejection of his wife is reflected in the dramatic utterance, "Recede a me, uxor," found in the last line of the first and third stanzas. The wife's dismay at her dismissal is expressed movingly in the refrain of the second and fourth stanzas, "Dulcis jugalis meus."

Contemporary with Columba, Brendan, and Comgall was a sixth-century Welsh ecclesiastic, the "Blessed Saturninus," whose headstone yields this interesting inscription:

HIC BEATVS [. . .] SATVRNINVS
SE[PVLTVS I]ACIT
ET SVA SA[NCTA ?] CONIVX PA . . . [58]

The attitude of the "first order" of Irish saints toward the problem of women behind monastic walls is reported in the *Catalogus sanctorum Hiberniae,* composed probably in the ninth or tenth century: "Mulierum administrationem et consortia non respuebant, quia super petram Christum fundati ventum temptationis non timebant."[59] Of the "second order" it is recorded: "Mulierum quoque consortia ac administrationes fugiebant, atque a monasteriis suis eas excludebant."[60] However, the *Martyrology of Oengus* offers an extreme version of a test sometimes applied to the holy man: "Now two maidens with pointed breasts used to lie with him every night that the battle with the Devil might be the greater for him."[61] The ordeal is similar to one undergone by King Aldfrith's friend, Aldhelm, whose early tutelage was at the hands of Maildulph, the Irish founder of Malmesbury.[62]

Although there are no documents to corroborate the existence of such a test in Irish-founded Northumbrian monasteries,[63] it is significant that the author of the late seventh-century *Penitential of Theodore* admitted to the problem raised by the presence of women in northern monasteries. He writes: "Non licet viris feminas habere monachas neque feminis viros; tamen nos non destruamus illud quod consuetudo est in hac terra."[64]

Although he did not use it in his chapter given over to the life of St. Fursa (*H. E.* III, 19), Bede probably knew the story of how the Irish Fursa had befriended a clerk who had loved St. Molaisse's handmaid, only to see her die in childbirth.[65] Seeing the lover's wattle hut built beside the disgraced nun's grave, Fursa questions Molaisse and learns of the tragedy. Thanks to his intervention, the nun's body is transferred to sanctified ground, and the clerk accompanies St. Fursa on his mission to convert East Anglia *circa* 636.

It is reasonable to assume that many Northumbrian converts in Irish-fathered monasteries like Lindisfarne knew also the touching tale of Líadan and Cuirithir told in ninth-century Irish and preserved in two sixteenth-century manuscripts.[66] In the prose portion of the tale, we are led to believe that "after Líadan had promised to marry Cuirithir, she decided to become a nun. Cuirithir thereupon became a monk."[67] In words

frankly reflecting the grief of separation, Líadan, hearing of
her lover's exile, cries:

> I am Líadan; I loved Cuirithir; this is as true as
> anything told.

> For a short time I was in the company of Cuirithir;
> to be with me was profitable to him.

> Forest music used to sing to me beside Cuirithir,
> together with the sound of the fierce sea.

> I should have thought that no arrangement I might
> make would have vexed Cuirithir in regard to me.

> Conceal it not: he was my heart's love, even though I
> should love all others besides.

> A roar of fire has split my heart; without him for certain
> it will not live.[68]

It will be recalled that the exile motif is strong in the *Wife's
Lament* of the Exeter Book where it is the wife who suffers in
exile:

> Ic þis giedd wrece bi me ful geomorre,
> minre sylfre sið. Ic þaet secgan maeg,
> hwaet ic yrmþa gebad, siþþan ic up weox,
> niwes oþþe ealdes, no ma þonne nu.
> A ic wite wonn minra wraecsiþa.                   ll. 1–5

> (In solitude I sing this lonely song
> About my fate; and truly can I say
> That of the ills encountered since my youth,
> Ills new and old, most grievous far is this—
> Sorrows of endless exile I endure!)[69]

That the strongest bond of affection had held wife and husband
together before their separation is underlined by poignant words:

> Bliþe gebaero ful oft wit beotedan
> þaet unc ne gedaelde nemne deað ana
> owiht elles; eft is þaet onhworfen,
> is nu. . . .                                        ll. 21–24

> (Often we promised faithfully that love
> Should last with life, that separation naught
> But death alone should bring—how different now!)[70]

In addition to the tale of *Líadan and Cuirithir* there is the story of Crinog that may have circulated widely among the monasteries in the Lindisfarne sphere of influence. As told in a tenth-century Irish manuscript it sings the praise of an ecclesiastic's consort:

> Since then you have slept with four men after me,
> Without folly or falling away:
> I know, I hear it on all sides,
> You are pure, without sin from man.
>
> At last, after weary wanderings,
> You have come to me again,
> Darkness of age has settled on your face:
> Sinless your life draws near its end.
>
> You are still dear to me, faultless one,
> You shall have welcome from me without stint:
> You will not let us be drowned in torment;
> We will earnestly practice devotion with you.[71]

A knowledge of the theme of the enforced separation of secular lovers along with an awareness of the problem posed by the Irish ecclesiastical consort tradition would have been possessed by the eighth-century Northumbrian poet, particularly if he himself belonged to a *familia*. Early Irish penitentials, developed independently of Continental types by contemporaries of Columba, exerted deep and lasting influence on both monks and the secular penitents who came to the monasteries for help and guidance.[72] In these Irish handbooks of penance, widely used and copied in Northumbria after 635, exile was a commonly prescribed punishment for those who fell prey to the lust of the flesh.[73] To a bilingual patron of Insular learning like King Aldfrith, friend of Columba's biographer, Adamnan, the Old English poet's utilization of the lovers' exile motif in a poem such as the *Wife's Lament* was perfectly understandable. In an Insular version of the *Dies Irae*, probably composed by Columba of Iona, appear four concluding lines *not* found in the Vulgate:

> in quo cessabit mulierum
> amor et desiderium
> hominumque contentio
> mundi huius et cupido.

(The love of women's over,
 And ended is desire,
 Man's strife with men is quiet,
 And the world lusts no more.) [74]

Periculosae plenum opus aleae
Tractas et incedis per ignes
Suppositos cineri doloso.
Horace

*Chapter*
# VIII

## A NOTE
## IN EPILOGUE

Obviously the long-standing, loose cultural ties between Ireland
and Britain were made much firmer by the dynamic expansion
of Irish monasticism. Although the scant thirteen miles of sea
separating the Antrim coast from the Mull of Cantyre probably
would have assured the sporadic passage of exiles, fugitives,
settlers, raiders, and slavers, the arrival in the Highland Zone
of Britain during the sixth century of famous individual Irish
missionary monks signaled an end to haphazard contact. The
visits of ecclesiastics like Finnian of Clonard, Brendan of Clonfert, Comgall of Bangor, and Ciaran of Clonmacnoise, first attested to in Irish hagiography, are memorialized in *Scotia Minor*
—the lesser Ireland—by church dedications, charms, songs, and
incantations. But it was under the leadership of Columba of
Iona that *peregrinatio* assumed a purpose and proselytism took
on a plan; it is his achievement in founding Iona in the Hebrides
that stands above all the rest; and it is this achievement which
gave impetus to the founding, and informed the development,
of a great Northumbrian monastery. This was Lindisfarne—
Colum's other island.

Under Aidan's hand and in the Columban tradition, a second
Iona arose in Northumbria to father other monasteries, to ce-

ment relations between monks at Lindisfarne and kings at neighboring Bamburgh, to act as a broad channel of Irish influence in Northumbria through the years of the shattering Viking raids, and to assume a status as the citadel of what can be called Insular humanism. Lindisfarne offered a regimen of work and prayer that attracted many Northumbrian converts, among them men of royal blood as well as commoners. Behind its *vallum* worked scribes, illuminators, and stonecutters, whose output reflects the persistent strength of Irish influence at Lindisfarne long after the Council of Whitby had met in 664, a date too long accepted as the *terminus ad quem* for such influence.

To Ireland, often by way of Iona, traveled many of Lindisfarne's sons, some as celebrated as King Aldfrith of Northumbria, whose first contact with Irish monastic culture had come during his stay at Iona as a prince-in-exile. Among the anonymous Northumbrian visitors to Ireland mentioned by Bede may have been the makers of some of Old English literature. In Irish monasteries such as Clonfert, Clonmacnoise, and Clonard, Aldfrith and his countrymen learned new respect for the mystery of the Gospel, acquainted themselves with the surviving residue of classical literature, and were regaled with a vast store of stories and poems both secular and ecclesiastical.

But it is chiefly from an examination of the manuscripts produced in scriptoria of Ireland and Lindisfarne that we gain knowledge of the degree of contact between monks and converts. Paleographical studies show Northumbrian scribes capable of mastering two distinctive scripts developed in Irish monasteries and introduced to Northumbria through Lindisfarne. In the Antiphonary of Bangor, the Cathach of Columba, and the Schaffhausen Adamnan is reflected, in its formative stage, an Insular culture that eventually produced magnificent Gospel codices and stone crosses at Lindisfarne. In the Book of Kells and the Lindisfarne Gospels there is afforded a chance to see inevitable differences in temperament, tone, and purpose between the Irish and Northumbrians. Yet never is there doubt as to the identity of the first teachers in Northumbrian scriptoria, and the

Irish-instituted Insular hand graces even the folios of the Old English Exeter Book of the tenth century.

From certain stone crosses of the Highland Zone, including fragments of those produced at Lindisfarne, comes more evidence of persistent Irish influence beyond the scriptoria. In the Ruthwell Cross with its motif of Christ standing on the beasts we are reminded again that Celtic Christianity was related to, but different from, Continental Christianity. Also, the involvement of Columba's name and deeds with the idea of the stone cross demonstrates the longevity of his influence in Insular cultural life.

Certain elegiac poems of the Exeter Book suggest the existence of an elegiac tradition that drew its inspiration largely from documents and traditions of the type funneled through Lindisfarne after 635. In the *Ruin* and the *Wife's Lament* there appear increments of this self-contained, self-sustained Insular literary tradition that incorporated materials from annals and chronicles, saints' lives, ascetic practices, and penitential prescriptions singularly non-Continental.

This portrayal of Lindisfarne as the primary source and promulgator of an Irish-sponsored Insular culture in Northumbria is meant in no way to diminish the Roman-Mediterranean contribution so well documented over the years. There can be no denial of the value of the infusion of Roman elements into the Northumbrian cultural stream at the hands of men like Hadrian, Theodore, and Benedict Biscop. But the truth needs restating that this infusion was accepted sometimes grudgingly by a flourishing and adaptable Anglo-Irish culture with its own ecclesiastical provenance and secular traditions. To hold that the Council of Whitby marks the superimposition of a Roman-Mediterranean pattern and the disappearance of the fruit of the Irish-Saxon synthesis is to confuse matters of ecclesiastical polity with matters of broad cultural interest and to ignore the evidence of paleography, hagiography, and archaeology.

Perhaps traditional *Keltologie* and *Anglistik* deserve to be supplemented, possibly even replaced by Celto-Saxon studies. If so, much remains to be done.[1] Certain saints and kings like

Columba, Cuthbert, and Aldfrith deserve biographies better than those now available. There must be a closer reading and sifting of the works of record-keepers, annalists, chroniclers, and hagiographers[2] for additional evidence of intercourse between Dark-Age Britain and Ireland. Manuscripts from scriptoria, particularly in Northumbria, call for scrutiny with the hope of establishing a particular pattern for their preparation and distribution at individual monasteries. The riddle of the source of certain illumination motifs in manuscripts demands solving, perhaps with closer reference to Byzantine materials. The handiwork of the stonecarver has yet to be thoroughly appraised. A full account of the learning to which Northumbrians were exposed in Irish monasteries has still to be written, probably with recourse to Continental library catalogs and closer investigation of the scholarship of Irishmen at Charlemagne's court. The question of possible direct Irish influence on the Old English storyteller needs to be re-opened and vigorous probing encouraged.[3]

New lines of investigation deserve to be followed. A comparative study of Old Irish and Old English law might be fruitful, as well as a comparison of Old Irish and Old English music, ecclesiastical and secular. There is also a need for a more thorough study of the impact of Celtic liturgical practices on Northumbria than any that has yet been undertaken.[4] More attention deserves to be paid to coin-hoards and what they may suggest about cultural contact between Celt, German, and Scandinavian. The study of magic and charms and their transmission from Ireland to Northumbria has only begun.[5] An examination of Celtic architectural survivals in the remains of Saxon churches, along with a continuing analysis of the jewelry, hanging bowls, and other implements in treasures like those at Sutton Hoo and St. Chad's Church is essential.

The examination of these and other Celtic aspects of Insular culture should best be undertaken by men who are relatively free of ancient national and religious prejudices, who concede that historians sometimes repeat one another more often than history repeats itself, and who deem it worth the risk to try breaking through an alleged cul-de-sac in hope of fruitful exploration and discovery.

# REFERENCE MATTER

# List of Abbots, Bishops, and Kings

## ABBOTS AND BISHOPS

| Iona | Lindisfarne |
|---|---|
| Columcille, 563 | Aidan, 635 |
| Baithene, 597 | Finan, 651 |
| Laisren, 600 | Colman, 661 |
| Fergna Brit, 605 | Tuda, 664 |
| Seghene, 623 | Eata, 678 |
| Suibhne, 652 | Cuthbert, 685 |
| Cuimine Ailbhe, 657 | Eadbert, 688 |
| Failbe, 669 | Eadfrid, 698 |
| Adamnan, 679 | Ethelwald, 724 |
| Conamhail, 704 | Cynewulf, 740 |
| Dunchadh, 710 | Higbald, 780 |
| Faelcu, 717 | |
| Cillene Fada, 724 | |
| Cilline Droicteach, 726 | |
| Slebhine, 752 | |
| Suibhne, 767 | |
| Breasal, 772 | |

KINGS

| *Northumbria* | *Mercia* |
|---|---|
| Ethelfrith, 593 | Cearl, 606 |
| Edwin, 617 | Penda, 626 |
| Eanfrid, in Bernicia ⎱ 633 | Peada (under Oswy of |
| Osric, in Deira ⎰ | Northumbria), 655 |
| Oswald, 634 | Wulfhere, 658 |
| Oswy, in Bernicia ⎱ 641 | Ethelred, 675 |
| Oswin, in Deira ⎰ | Cemred, 704 |
| Oswy, 651 | Ceolred, 709 |
| Egfrid, 671 | Ethelbald, 716 |
| Aldfrith, 685 | Beornred, 757 |
| Eadwulf, 705 | Offa, 757 |
| Osred, 706 | Ecgfrith, 796 |
| Cenred, 716 | Coenwulf, 796 |
| Osric, 718 | |
| Ceolwulf, 729 | |
| Eadbert, 737 | |
| Oswulf, 758 | |
| Moll Aethelwald, 759 | |
| Alchred, 765 | |
| Aethelred, 774 | |
| Aelfwald, 778 | |
| Osred, 789 | |
| Aethelred, 790 | |
| Oswald, 796 | |
| Eardwulf, 796 | |

# Notes

CHAPTER I

1 *A Celtic Miscellany*, trans. Kenneth H. Jackson (Cambridge, Mass., 1951), pp. 12, 153; Myles Dillon, "The Archaism of Irish Tradition," *Proceedings of the British Academy*, XXXIII (1947), 245–64.

2 Whitley Stokes, "The Adventures of St. Columba's Clerics," *Revue Celtique*, XXVI (1905), pp. 130–70. Coincidences with the *Divine Comedy* are pointed out. The clerics see a whirlpool in the midst of a fiery river that whirls souls of survivors around (*Inf.* VII, 22); they watch hosts of fiends beating sinners on the heads with fiery maces (*Inf.* XVIII, 35). See also Charles S. Boswell, *An Irish Precursor of Dante* (London, 1908). See Howard R. Patch, *The Other World* (Cambridge, Mass., 1950), pp. 27–59 for a survey of medieval Irish adventures in wonderland. For a contemporary poet's interest in these fanciful journeys see W. H. Auden's *The Enchafèd Flood* (New York, 1950), pp. 22–23, where the island imagery in Tennyson's "Voyage of Maeldune" is examined.

3 Roger, *L'Enseignement des lettres classiques*, pp. 48–169; Kuno Meyer, *Learning in Ireland in the Fifth Century and the Transmission of Letters* (Dublin, 1913), p. 6 *et seq.;* also, Gougaud, *Christianity in Celtic Lands*, pp. 242–43; more recently Nora K. Chadwick, "Intellectual Contacts between Britain and Gaul in

101

the Fifth Century," in *Studies in Early British History*, ed. Chadwick, pp. 189–253. See especially Nora K. Chadwick, *Poetry and Letters in Early Christian Gaul* (London, 1955), p. 326; also James Carney, "The Impact of Christianity," in *Early Irish Society*, ed. Myles Dillon (Dublin, 1954), pp. 66–72. Possible Irish contact with Roman techniques of enameling at Namur possibly as early as the third century is suggested by Françoise Henry, "Irish Enamels of the Dark Age and their Relation to Cloisonné Techniques," in *Dark-Age Britain*, ed. Harden, pp. 71–86.

4 *Hisperica Famina*, ed. Jenkinson, p. xi. For perceptive comments on certain selections in *Hisperica Famina*, see Browne, *British Latin Selections*, pp. 3–5. See also Phillip W. Damon, "The Meaning of the *Hisperica Famina*," *American Journal of Philology*, LXXIV (1953), 398–406.

5 Kenney, *Sources*, I, 164–65.

6 *Ibid.*, pp. 260–61.

7 Slover, in Univ. of Texas *Studies in English*, No. 6, pp. 14–15, 27–32. For a fresh survey of St. Patrick and his place in the history of fifth-century Britain and Ireland see *Saint Patrick*, ed. John Ryan (Dublin, 1958). Archaeological evidence from Lydney in Gloucestershire points to the existence of a "community in the late fourth century which worshipped a god with close Irish affinities."—Peter Blair, *An Introduction to Anglo-Saxon England* (Cambridge, 1956), p. 5.

8 For Plummer's summary of the facts regarding the founding of Candida Casa and other estimates of its influence, see *Ven. Baedae Hist. eccl.*, ed. Plummer, II, 128; *History of the Church of Ireland*, ed. Phillips, I, 72–73; also Knight, *Archaeological Light*, I, 113–27. William D. Simpson, *Saint Ninian and the Origins of the Christian Church in Scotland* (Edinburgh, 1940), stresses that Ninian lived and worked in an area around the Solway Basin that was very much Romanized although without Roman protection when Candida Casa was founded in 397.

9 *Baedae Opera historica*, trans. King, I, 341. All subsequent *H. E.* references are to this edition. See Wilhelm Levison, "An Eighth Century Poem on St. Ninian," *Antiquity*, XIV (1940), p. 289. Perhaps the poet was obliging the Saxon community here in the eighth century "by establishing and increasing the fame of the ancient founder."

10 See Ryan, *Irish Monasticism*, pp. 105–6.

11 *Lives of Saint Ninian and Saint Kentigern*, ed. and trans. Alexander P. Forbes (Edinburgh, 1874), p. 11.

12 Kenney, *Sources*, I, 178–79. See also Bowen, *Settlements of the Celtic Saints*, p. 60: "From this base [Menevia] St. David

was in contact with Celtic Christianity in Southern Ireland, in south-western England and in Brittany."

13  Slover, in Univ. of Texas *Studies in English*, No. 7, pp. 8–10. For an analysis of the place of the St. David tradition in intercourse between early Ireland and western Britain, see Nora K. Chadwick, "Intellectual Life in West Wales in the Last Days of the Celtic Church," in *Studies in the Early British Church*, ed. Chadwick, pp. 130–33 *et seq.*

14  The views of Plummer and Stokes on the credibility and usefulness of saints' lives in investigations of this type are recommended. See *Vit. Sanct. Hib.*, ed. Plummer, I, xci; and *Lives of Saints*, ed. Stokes, pp. xci–xcii, xcv.

15  *Lives of Saints*, ed. Stokes, p. 222.

16  *Ibid.*, p. 224. See also Kathleen Hughes, "The Historical Value of the Lives of St. Finnian of Clonard," *English Historical Review*, LXIX (1954), 353–72.

17  Kenney, *Sources*, I, 279–80.

18  *Vit. Sanct. Hib.*, ed. Plummer, II, 214.

19  *Ibid.*, pp. 240–41.

20  Concerning the evidence of church dedications see Bowen, *Settlements of the Celtic Saints*, p. 2; Owen Chadwick, "The Evidence of Dedications in the Early History of the Welsh Church," in *Studies in Early British History*, ed. Chadwick, pp. 173, 175, 182, 185.

21  Mackinlay, *Ancient Church Dedications*, II, 80.

22  *Ibid.*, p. 81.

23  *Ibid.*, pp. 82, 83.

24  A transposition brought about through phonological change. The sequence was probably *f* to *v* to *w*.

25  Slover, in Univ. of Texas *Studies in English*, No. 7, p. 25.

26  *Chronicum Scotorum*, ed. William M. Hennessy, Rolls Series (London, 1866), p. 145.

27  *Early Sources of Scottish History*, ed. Anderson, I, 19.

28  Myles Dillon, *Early Irish Literature* (Chicago, 1948), p. 124.

29  See Carl Selmer, "The Vernacular Translations of the *Navigatio Sancti Brendani*: A Bibliographical Study," *Mediaeval Studies*, XVIII (1956), 145–57.

30  *Lives of Saints*, ed. Stokes, p. 253. As late as 1721 a voyage in quest of the Island of St. Brendan was undertaken. See also T. J. Westropp, "Brasil and the Legendary Islands of the North Atlantic," *Proceedings of the Royal Irish Academy*, XXX (1912), 223–60.

31  Mackinlay, *Ancient Church Dedications*, II, 67.

32  *Ibid.*, pp. 68, 69.

33  *Carmina Gadelica,* ed. Carmichael, I, 259.
34  *Ibid.,* IV, 41.
35  *Lives of Saints,* ed. Stokes, p. 267.
36  *Vit. Sanct. Hib.,* ed. Plummer, I, 206.
37  Kenney, *Sources,* I, 377–78.
38  *The War of the Gaedhil with the Gaill,* ed. and trans. James H.
    Todd, Rolls Series (London, 1867), p. 226.
39  Mackinlay, *Ancient Church Dedications,* II, 86–87.
40  *Carmina Gadelica,* ed. Carmichael, II, 55.
41  *Early Sources,* ed. Anderson, I, 52–53.
42  *Adamnani Vita S. Columbae,* ed. Fowler, p. 175.
43  Mackinlay, *Ancient Church Dedications,* II, 64.
44  *Ibid.,* p. 65.
45  Slover, in Univ. of Texas *Studies in English,* No. 7, pp. 39–40.
46  *Bethada Náem nÉrenn,* ed. and trans. Charles Plummer (Ox-
    ford, 1922), II, 126.
47  *A Dictionary of Saints,* ed. Donald Attwater (London, 1938),
    pp. 35–36.
48  Mackinlay, *Ancient Church Dedications,* II, 88.
49  *Lives of Saints,* ed. Stokes, p. 171. The best modern biography
    of St. Columba is by Lucy Menzies, *St. Columba of Iona* (Lon-
    don and New York, 1920). See also William D. Simpson, *The
    Celtic Church in Scotland* (Aberdeen, 1935).
50  *Lives of Saints,* ed. Stokes, p. 171.
51  *Ibid.,* p. 45.
52  *Félire Óengusso Céli Dé,* ed. Stokes, p. 149.
53  Derek J. Schove, "Visions in North-West Europe (A.D. 400–600)
    and Dated Auroral Displays," *Journal of the British Archaeolog-
    ical Association,* XIII (1950), p. 37.
54  *Ibid.:* "The event would seem to be dateable, and aurorae were
    evidently seen in Ireland within a few months, as contemporar-
    ies firmly believed the rays seen to the north were the angels
    carrying the soul of St. Columba to Heaven."
55  *Félire Óengusso Céli Dé,* ed. Stokes, p. 149.
56  Adamnan, *Life of St. Columba,* ed. Reeves, preface, *passim.*
57  *Ibid.,* p. xlviii. Apparent instances of bloody fights between mo-
    nastic communities are recorded in Irish annals. In 673 Clon-
    macnoise defeated Durrow. In a battle between Taghman and
    Ferns in 816, four hundred were slain. According to Reeves it
    was "not until 804, that the monastic communities of Ireland
    were formally exempted from military service." It is not likely
    that a reputation for brawling, earned or fictitious, detracted
    from the prestige of the first Irish missionaries to Scotland and
    Northumbria.

58 See Florence M. McNeill, *Iona: A History of the Island,* 4th ed. (London, 1954).
59 See J. Jeffrey Waddell, "The Chapel or Oratory of St. Columba at Iona," *Transactions of the Glasgow Archaeological Society,* New Series, X (1951), 55–59. Waddell gives a sketch of the chapel of St. Columba and states the belief that the oratory now seen there was built in Columba's time. See William J. Watson, "Early Irish Influences in Scotland," *Transactions of the Gaelic Society of Inverness,* XXXV (1929–30), 191.
60 Mackinlay, *Ancient Church Dedications,* II, 43–55.
61 *Carmina Gadelica,* ed. Carmichael, I, II, and IV *passim.*
62 William Mackenzie, "Gaelic Incantations, Charms, and Blessings in the Hebrides," *Transactions of the Gaelic Society of Inverness,* XVIII (1891–92), 154, 168–69. In this connection see Godfrid Storms, *Anglo-Saxon Magic* (The Hague, 1948), pp. 70–71: "If a horse is elf-shot, or other cattle, take dock seed and Irish (OE *seyttisc*) wax, have a priest sing twelve masses over them. . . ." See also p. 303, where part of an incantation for a charm against a worm appears to be Irish. See also Howard Meroney, "Irish in Old English Charms," *Speculum,* XX (1945), 172–82.
63 *Baedae Opera historica,* trans. King, I, 339.
64 Osbert G. S. Crawford, "Iona," *Antiquity,* VII (1933), 453–67.
65 Robert B. K. Stevenson, "The Iona Hoard of Anglo-Saxon Coins," *Numismatic Chronicle,* XI (1951), 68–90, and the same author's "A Hoard of Anglo-Saxon Coins Found at Iona Abbey," *Proceedings of the Society of Antiquaries of Scotland,* LXXXV (1953), 170–72.
66 See *Johnson's Journey to the Western Islands of Scotland and Boswell's Journal of a Tour to the Hebrides,* ed. R. W. Chapman (Oxford, 1924), p. 135.
67 *Boswell's Journal of a Tour to the Hebrides,* eds. F. A. Pottle and C. H. Bennett (New York, 1936), pp. 334–36.
68 See Wordsworth's poem "Iona," *The Poetical Works of Wordsworth,* ed. Thomas Hutchinson (London, 1932), p. 474.
69 See George Calder, *A Gaelic Grammar* (Glasgow, 1923), pp. 144–45. From *Brendan* come: *Mac gille Bhrā, Mac gille Bhrāi, Mac Gillivray;* from *Colum* [*Columba*]: *Mac Gille Calum, Maol Calum, Malcolm, Malcolmson;* from *Comgán* [*Kevin*]: *Mac-Cowan, Cowan;* from *Ciaran*: *MacKerron;* from *Adamnan*: *Mac Lagan.*
70 To read of John Millington Synge's adventures in this craft during his Aran Islands stay is to call up a new respect for the courage of the early ecclesiastical voyagers.—*The Aran Islands* (Boston, 1911). This amazingly seaworthy vessel exists today

with minor modifications much as it has existed since Caesar's time, a broad, ovate, latticed framework in the form of a shallow wide-mouthed basket covered with calico, waterproofed outside with pitch and tar. See James Hornell, *British Coracles and Irish Curraghs* (London, 1938). Though humble compared with the Anglo-Saxon Sutton Hoo ship, the curragh has had a role in maintaining economic and cultural ties between Ireland, Britain, Scotland, and the Western Islands which cannot be overemphasized. See particularly Thomas C. Lethbridge, *Merlin's Island* (London, 1948), and his *Herdsmen and Hermits* (Cambridge, 1950), for an archaeologist's appraisal of the curragh's importance. G. J. Marcus, "The Scotic Curach," *Scottish Gaelic Studies*, VII, Pt. 2 (1953), 105–14, reviews allusions to this remarkable craft in saints' lives and annals. He believes the curragh's large square sail and keel make it "a true sailing ship." See the same author's "Factors in Early Celtic Navigation," *Études Celtiques*, VI (1953–54), 312–27.

71 See Fox, *Personality of Britain*, p. 87: "South of the Forth-Clyde isthmus the island consists of two parts, the Highland Zone to the west and the Lowland Zone to the east. A diagonal line drawn from Teesmouth (Durham) to Torquay (Devon) roughly indicates the boundary of the two areas."

CHAPTER II

1 For an air view of Lindisfarne, see David Knowles and J. K. St. Joseph, *Monastic Sites from the Air* (Cambridge, 1952), pp. 40–41.

2 Bamburgh was founded in 547 by King Ida. See *Henrici archidiaconi huntendunensis Historia Anglorum*, ed. Thomas Arnold, Rolls Series (London, 1879), p. 50. It was attacked in 866–67 by the Danes and again in 993. See G. T. Clark, "Bamburgh Castle," *Archaeological Journal*, XLVI (1889), 93–113.

3 The route can be traced on the Ordnance Survey's North Sheet of *The Map of Britain in the Dark Ages* (Southampton, 1938); see also Ivan D. Margary, *Roman Roads in Britain*, (London, 1957), II, 216, and appended map. Irish missionaries to Northumbria first met the remnants of Roman civilization in forts, camps, signal stations, roads, and frontier walls forming its outer periphery. See Kenneth Steer, "Roman Scotland," *Scottish Historical Review*, XXXIII (1954), 115–28.

4 Knight, *Archaeological Light*, II, 113–14.

5 For the ground plan of an Irish monastery possibly modeled after Iona, see Lawlor, *Monastery of St. Mochaoi*, p. 113 and appended map. See Angus Graham, "Archaeological Gleanings from

Dark-Age Records," *Proceedings of the Society of Antiquaries of Scotland,* LXXXV (1953), 64–91.

6 Bede's account of this event is in *H. E.* III, 2. See also J. M. Winmill, "Iona and Lindisfarne," *Irish Ecclesiastical Record,* 5th Series, LXXX (1953), 106–14.

7 Raine, *History and Antiquities,* p. 2. See also Edmund Craster, "The Patrimony of St. Cuthbert," *English Historical Review,* LXIX (1954), 178–79.

8 Symeon of Durham, *Opera omnia,* ed. Arnold, I, 200.

9 Dugdale, *Monasticon Anglicanum,* I, 221.

10 Oswald's piety was to bring him fame in the form of cult worship in northern Italy and Switzerland. See Eric P. Baker, "St. Oswald and His Church at Zug," *Archaeologia,* XCIII (1949), 121–23, and the same author's "The Cult of St. Oswald in Northern Italy," *Archaeologia,* XCIV (1951), 167–94. The efficacy of his name and relics comes close to matching that of St. Columba's. See Wilfrid Bonser, "The Magic of St. Oswald," *Antiquity,* IX (1935), 418–23.

11 *Baedae Opera historica,* trans. King, I, 349.

12 *Ibid.,* pp. 403–5.

13 *Ibid.,* p. 483.

14 *Ibid.,* p. 493. Like Iona, Lindisfarne could be classified as one of the *monasteria Scottorum,* governed by Irishmen and with a majority of Irish monks among their inmates. See Gougaud, *Christianity in Celtic Lands,* p. 157.

15 *The Buik of the Croniclis of Scotland; or a Metrical Version of the History of Hector Boece,* ed. William B. Turnbull, Rolls Series (London, 1858), II, 309–10.

16 *Lestorie des Engles solum La Translacion Maistre Geffrei Gaimar,* eds. Thomas Duffus Hardy and Charles T. Martin, Rolls Series (London, 1889), II, 40–42.

17 *The Chronicle of Florence of Worcester with the Two Continuations,* trans. Thomas Forester (London, 1854), p. 15.

18 Bertram Colgrave, "The Post-Bedan Miracles and Translations of St. Cuthbert," in *The Early Cultures of North-west Europe,* eds. Bruce Dickins and Cyril Fox (Cambridge, 1950), pp. 314–16.

19 Not without discord, however. Bede reports (*H. E.* IV, 4) that the Irish members of Mayo were inclined to wander abroad in the summer leaving the harvest to the English. Colman solved the problem by establishing a separate monastery for the English. Colman supposedly took some of Aidan's bones to Iona with him. See *The Life of Bishop Wilfrid by Eddius Stephanus,* ed. and trans. B. Colgrave (Cambridge, 1927), p. 157.

20 *Baedae Opera historica,* trans. King, I, 479.

21 *Matthaei Parisiensis, monachi Sancti Albani, Chronica majora,* ed. Henry R. Luard, Rolls Series (London, 1872), I, 294. According to the chroniclers its victims turned yellow. Possibly it was a particularly virulent form of typhus.

22 Bede's well-known statement on this *en masse* visit to Ireland by Northumbrian converts is found in *H. E.* III, 27.

23 According to William of Malmesbury, Wilfrid was indebted to Lindisfarne for his early schooling.—*De gest. pont.,* p. 212.

24 *Baedae Opera historica,* trans. King, I, 481.

25 A case has been made for Cuthbert's Irish lineage. See *Rites of Durham,* Surtees Society, CVII (Durham, 1903), 63, where the entry has Cuthbert "descended of the blood Royal of the kings of Ireland." See also Irene P. McKeehan, "The Book of the Nativity of St. Cuthbert," *PMLA,* XLVIII (1933), 981–99. However, see Paul Grosjean, "The Alleged Irish Origin of St. Cuthbert," in *The Relics of St. Cuthbert,* ed. C. F. Battiscombe (Oxford, 1956), pp. 144–54.

26 Ordericus Vitalis, *The Ecclesiastical History of England and Normandy,* trans. Thomas Forester (London, 1853), I, 125. His reputation rests partially on such ascetic acts as standing up to his loins in icy water, and leaving his shoes on from one Maundy Thursday to another when foot-washing rites took place. See Edmund Craster, "The Miracles of St. Cuthbert at Farne," *Analecta Bollandiana,* LXX (1952), 5–19.

27 *The Victoria History of the County of Durham,* ed. William Page (London, 1905), I, 241–44.

28 See Chapter V, below, for an account of Irish influence in the Gospels of Lindisfarne and other MSS prepared in northern scriptoria.

29 Raine, *History and Antiquities,* p. 68. See my Chapter VI, below, for Irish influence reflected in the Ruthwell and Bewcastle Crosses.

30 This is the Ceolwulf to whom Bede dedicated the *Historia Ecclesiastica.* In 731 he was forced into a monastery and tonsured. Although restored to his throne within a year, he voluntarily joined the *familia* at Lindisfarne in 737. He was buried at Lindisfarne near St. Cuthbert in 760. Irish annals refer to his tonsuring in entries under the years 730 and 731. Like King Aldfrith he seems to have had an Irish name—*Eochaid.*

31 An event recorded in *Annales Lindisfarnenses*: "793. 6 Iduum Iuniarum vastata est a paganis Lindisfarnensis aecclesia. Set sequenti anno omnes perierunt."—*Monum. Germ. Hist., Scriptorum,* XIX, ed. Georg H. Pertz (Hanover, 1866), p. 505.

32 *Alcvini . . . Epistolae, MGH, Epist.* IV, 57, 183. See Roland M.

Frye, "Christ and Ingeld," *Theology Today*, XI (1954–55), 225–32.

33  *Baedae Opera historica,* trans. King, I, 337, 339.

34  Dugdale, *Monasticon Anglicanum,* I, 342.

35  *Ibid.,* p. 405.

36  Francis P. Magoun, Jr., "Bede's Story of Caedman: The Case History of an Anglo-Saxon Oral Singer," *Speculum,* XXX (1955), 49–63. See G. Shepherd, "The Prophetic Caedmon," *Review of English Studies,* V (1954), 113–14. Reference is made to Fursa of East Anglia, an Irish holy man who had seen visions of heaven and hell. Shepherd writes: " . . . this type of spiritual effort and this type of spiritual voyage are common features of mantic literature, particularly among the Celts." See also *Early Irish Lyrics,* ed. Murphy, pp. 92–106.

37  Dugdale, *Monasticon Anglicanum,* II, 131.

38  *Ibid.,* III, 302.

39  *Baedae Opera historica,* trans. King, I, 455.

40  *Ibid.,* II, 167.

41  *Ibid.,* p. 267.

42  *Ibid.,* p. 17.

43  Dugdale, *Monasticon Anglicanum,* VI, 1626.

44  No appraisal of the impact of Irish monasticism on northern Britain should ignore completely Irish elements in the founding traditions of such southern monasteries as Glastonbury, Abingdon, and Malmesbury. St. Patrick's name is tied closely to the early history of Glastonbury.—Dugdale, *Monasticon Anglicanum,* I, 1. A tenth-century life of St. Dunstan supplies the most reliable reference to Irish influence at Glastonbury.—*Memorials of St. Dunstan, Archbishop of Canterbury,* ed. William M. Stubbs, Rolls Series (London, 1874), pp. 10–11. William of Malmesbury used a considerable number of Irish traditions connected with Glastonbury in his *De antiquitate Glastoniensis ecclesiae,* in *Patrologie cursus completus,* Series Latina, ed. J. P. Migne (1855), CLXXIX, cols. 1681–1734. See C. H. Slover, "William of Malmesbury and the Irish," *Speculum,* II (1927), 274; also his "Glastonbury Abbey and the Fusing of English Literary Culture," *Speculum,* X (1935), 147–60. Glastonbury's tradition of a visit by Columba of Iona was exploited by its historians in the twelfth century as was the story that the bones of Aidan were brought to Glastonbury by Tican, abbot of Whitby in 754, as he fled before oncoming Scandinavian raiders.

  The founding of Abingdon in Berkshire is credited by one source to an Irish monk named Abbanan or Abban, who called his monastery "Abbendun" and ruled over three hundred monks before returning to Ireland.—*Chronicon monasterii de Abingdon,* ed. Joseph Stevenson, Rolls Series (London, 1858), I, 2–3. However, Dugdale writes that Abingdon was founded in 675 by "Cysse, or Cyssa, one of the viceroys of Kinwine."—*Monasticon Anglicanum,* I, 505.

Malmesbury in Wiltshire was founded before 640, according to William of Malmesbury, by an Irish monk named Maildulph. Place-name evidence shows the original form of Malmesbury to have been *Maldufesburg.*—Eilert Ekwall, *The Concise Oxford Dictionary of English Place Names* (Oxford, 1936), p. 297. Maildulph's most talented pupil was Aldhelm, who acknowledged his own debt to Irish training in a letter to Eahfrid (possibly King Aldfrith), a contemporary who had gone directly to Ireland to receive instruction.

Bede tells of the founding of Bosham in Sussex by an Irishman named Dicul (*H. E.* IV, 13) and of the founding of Cnobheresburg by Fursa who arrived from Ireland between 630 and 648 (*H. E.* III, 19).

45  *Aedilvulfi Carmen, MGH, Poet. Latin. Medii Aevi,* I, 582–604.

46  Egbert's story is taken up again in *H. E.* V, 9, where we learn that he desires to evangelize Germany, but is prevented by a vision. Instrumental in sending Wilbrord to Germany, he later goes to Iona to "reform" Columba's monastery, where he dies in 728. In Irish annals he is called "Christ's knight."

47  *Aedilvulfi Carmen, MGH, Poet. Latin. Medii Aevi,* I, 589–91.

48  The term is used by Sean O'Faolain, *The Irish* (New York, 1949), p. 37. He sees the Irish up to the eleventh century fulfilling their genius through a "technique of dispersion and disconnection" as opposed to the "corporate technique of living" practiced by the Romans and Normans. The Irish monastic church of the sixth century was a strong manifestation of this tradition of decentralization, and practices stemming from it survived in Northumbria long after the Council of Whitby in 664. The Council of Hertford (673) directed that no bishop be allowed to intrude himself into another's diocese, that monks not move from one monastery to another without permission of their abbots, and that clerks or scholars be forbidden to wander without authorizing letters from their bishops.—*Councils and Ecclesiastical Documents,* eds. Haddan and Stubbs, III, 118–21. The seventh-century *Penitential of Theodore* proclaimed the excommunication of all those ordained by British or Irish bishops who refused to conform to the Roman practice regarding the celebration of Easter and the tonsure.—John L. G. Meissner, *The Celtic Church in England* (London, 1929), p. 201. As late as 816 the Council of

Celchyth declared that "no one of Irish race be allowed to exercise the sacred ministry in anyone's diocese . . . because it is uncertain to us, by whom, or whether indeed by anybody, they were ordained."—Meissner, *Celtic Church in England,* p. 202; *Councils and Ecclesiastical Documents,* eds. Haddan and Stubbs, III, 581.

49 *Exeter Book,* Part II, ed. Mackie, pp. 3–5.
50 *Ibid.,* p. 27.
51 *Ibid.,* pp. 43, 45.
52 *Ibid.,* pp. 89, 91, 93.

CHAPTER III

1 In *Vita S. Columbae* (II, 47) Adamnan reports "et in Saxonia, regem Aldfridum visitantes amicum. . . . "—Adamnan, *Life of St. Columba,* ed. Reeves, pp. 191, cli.

The widely known decisions involving ecclesiastical polity made at Whitby too long have obscured or overshadowed the fact that Irish *cultural* influence did not end in 664. As for the events at Whitby, John Ryan reminds us of some overlooked truths. The term *synod* is not a proper one to describe what was actually a conference called by a king and attended by only three bishops. Had it been a true synod, the bishops would have voted, in this case assuring a victory for Iona since two of the three were Irish. As it was, Oswy convened the group on his own responsibility and was alone responsible for the outcome. Although much has been made of the settlement of the Easter date controversy in favor of Rome, this system had been adopted by Rome "hardly more than three generations before" and "had been adopted throughout a half at least of Ireland before Aidan ever set foot in Northumbria." Ryan goes on to point out that from 664 until Bede's time, there is no evidence for a superior Roman or Benedictine learning in Northumbria from which the Irish could learn much that they did not already know. Ryan notes that of the Roman organizers of the north neither Biscop, Wilfrid, Theodore, nor Hadrian was a writer; neither Biscop nor Wilfrid was a teacher. See John Ryan, "Irish Learning in the Seventh Century," *Journal of the Royal Society of Antiquaries of Ireland,* LXXX (1950), 164–71. See also Laistner, *Thought and Letters in Western Europe,* Chap. V, for a summary of the activity of Irish and English scholars and missionaries up to the year of Bede's death.

2 Thomas Duffus Hardy, *Descriptive Catalogue of Materials Relating to the History of Britain and Ireland,* Rolls Series (London, 1862), I, Pt. I, 384.

3 *Baedae Opera historica,* trans. King, II, 165 and 429. See also
  *Ven. Baedae Hist. eccl.,* ed. Plummer, II, 263–64. Aldfrith's residence in Ireland is attested to by William of Malmesbury in *De
  gestis regum Anglorum,* ed. William Stubbs, Rolls Series (London, 1887), I, 57. See also Adamnan, *Life of Saint Columba,* ed.
  Reeves, pp. 283–84.
4 Vernam E. Hull, "The Wise Sayings of Flann Fína (Aldfrith,
  King of Northumbria)," *Speculum,* IV (1929), 95–102. Hull's text
  of the "Wise Sayings of Flann Fína" is based on the version
  found in the fourteenth-century *Book of Lecan.* Hull writes:
  "even though Aldfrith was not the author of the various works
  assigned to him, it is significant that such a tradition should have
  existed in Ireland, and that the Irish should have ascribed to a
  Northumbrian prince three separate compositions in their own
  language."
5 The passage, *H. E.* III, 27, bears quoting in full: "There were in
  that same place at that time many nobles as well as common
  sort of English race, who in the time of the bishops Finan and
  Colman had left their native island and departed aside thither
  either to read sacred writings or to live more strictly. And
  certain of them forthwith bound themselves faithfully to the
  monastical life, while others wandering rather about the cells of
  such as taught gladly gave good heed to reading: all of whom
  the Scots entertained cheerfully and were forward to give them
  daily sustenance free, also books for reading and teaching without payment."—*Baedae Opera historica,* trans. King, I, 485–87.
6 *History of the Church of Ireland,* ed. Phillips, I, 220–21. For a
  translation of another version of Aldfrith's poem, see Cook, *Transactions of the Connecticut Society of Arts and Sciences,* XXV,
  300–301.
7 *Ibid.*
8 Ryan, *Irish Monasticism,* p. 266.
9 *Ibid.* Ryan, however, does not believe that the clan system governed selection of new abbots in all monasteries.
10 Skene, *Celtic Scotland,* II, 69.
11 Ryan, *Irish Monasticism,* pp. 272–74.
12 *Ibid.,* pp. 172–73.
13 Macalister, *Archaeology of Ireland,* p. 248.
14 *Ibid.,* p. 239. Kathleen Hughes states that the "scribal traditions
   and the financial stability of Kildare seem to have developed
   together," and that in the cases of Kildare, Clonmacnoise and
   Clonard material prosperity added to intellectual and spiritual
   stimulus assured the maintenance of a great scriptorium.—"The
   Distribution of Irish Scriptoria and Centres of Learning from 730

to 1111," in *Studies in the Early British Church,* ed. Chadwick, pp. 252–55.

15 See Ryan, *Irish Monasticism,* pp. 207–9. On Irish monastic rules governing Irish inmates and their Northumbrian visitors, see O'Curry, *Lectures on the Manuscript Materials,* pp. 374–75.

16 *Life of St. Declan of Ardmore and Life of St. Mochuda of Lismore,* ed. and trans. Patrick Power (London, 1914), p. 13. The upper and middle classes were suppliers of recruits for the monasteries.—Ryan, *Irish Monasticism,* pp. 200–201. Many of Columba's contemporaries were from the nobility. Others, like Mochua of Timahoe and Enda of Aran, were successful warriors before their entrance into monasteries.

17 Skene, *Celtic Scotland,* II, 71.

18 Ryan, *Irish Monasticism,* p. 363.

19 Lawlor, *Monastery of St. Mochaoi,* p. 144 and facing plate.

20 *Ibid.,* p. 146.

21 Adamnan, *De locis sanctis,* as quoted in *Vita S. Columbae,* ed. Fowler, p. 42, n. 3. On wax tablets in general and particularly their use by Irish and Anglo-Saxons, see Wattenbach, *Das Schriftwesen im Mittelalter,* pp. 44–74.

22 *Vita S. Columbae,* ed. Fowler, p. 111.

23 *Vit. Sanct. Hib.,* ed. Plummer, II, 143.

24 *Vita S. Columbae,* ed. Fowler, p. 159.

25 *Lives of Saints,* ed. Stokes, p. 110.

26 *Vit. Sanct. Hib.,* ed. Plummer, I, 160.

27 Hugh Graham, *The Early Irish Monastic Schools* (Dublin, 1923), pp. 101–5. See Wattenbach, *Das Schriftwesen im Mittelalter*: on the scriptorium, pp. 184, 370; on the stylus, p. 182 *et seq.*; on the pen, p. 189; on the ink, pp. 193–94; and on the vellum, p. 93 *et seq.*

28 *Vita S. Columbae,* ed. Fowler, p. 143. See also this entry in the life of St. Lasrian (d. 639): "pennam uero qua librum scribere posset minime habebat."—*Vit. Sanct. Hib.,* ed. Plummer, II, 135.

29 Adamnan, *Life of Saint Columba,* ed. Reeves, pp. 20–21. On the use of the inkhorn in the medieval scriptorium, see Wattenbach, *Das Schriftwesen im Mittelalter,* pp. 201–3.

30 *Vit. Sanct. Hib.,* ed. Plummer, II, 233, 135; I, 252.

31 *Ibid.,* I, 58–59: "Sanctissima virgo Scletha filia Mec Chier misit nuncium ad sanctum Albeum, ut ipse mitteret scriptorem ad eam ad scribendos libros quatuor euangeliorum. Misit enim; et scriptor scripsit duos libros; et postea infirmitate correptus mortuus est." Also II, 24: "Beatus pater Cronanus quendam scriptorem rogauit ut sibi quatuor scriberet euangelia. Ipse iam scriptor Dymma uocabatur; et noluit scribere sancto nisi vno die. Et

ait ei sanctus: 'Scribe sine cessacione, usque dum sol tibi occubuerit.' Hoc scriptor promissit; et constituit ei sanctus sedem scribendo. Set gratia sancti Cronani diuinaque potencia radium solis quadraginta diebus et quadraginta noctibus in ipso loco semper esse fecit. Et nec scriptor lassus erat tanto tempore, nec tedium habuit, nec desiderio cibi uel potus siue sompni grauatus est."

32 *Ibid.*, II, 135. Frequent visiting on the part of abbots and lesser members of the *familia* furthered the exchange of scribes and manuscripts. See Ryan, *Irish Monasticism*, pp. 323–27.

33 *Vit. Sanct. Hib.*, ed. Plummer, II, 114–15. The quotation is from the life of St. Gerald of Mayo. See Chapter II, n. 19, above. Even in the thirteenth century, Irish annals refer to Mayo as *Magheo na Saxan* ("Mayo of the Saxons"). Mayo had an English leader in 768. Plummer infers from Alcuin's letter to its English monks that "whereas the Irish had formerly taught the English, now the positions are reversed."—*Ven. Baedae Hist. eccl.*, ed. Plummer, II, 210. Obviously Mayo was an important point for Irish-English cultural contact long after Whitby.

34 *Félire Óengusso Céli Dé*, ed. Stokes, p. 91.

35 *Ibid.*, p. 270.

36 *Ibid.*, p. 199.

37 *Annals of Ulster*, ed. Hennessy, I, 451. See also *The Annals of Clonmacnoise*, ed. Murphy, *passim*. See Hughes's admirable study of Irish scriptoria based on examination of scribes' obits in the annals.—*Studies in the Early British Church*, ed. Chadwick, pp. 243–72.

38 These seventh-century visitors from Northumbria are rightly regarded as sharers of the wandering scholar tradition along with their Irish hosts. See Helen Waddell, *The Wandering Scholars*, 7th ed. rev. (New York, 1934), p. 29.

39 Cook, in *Transactions of the Connecticut Society of Arts and Sciences*, XXV, 292–93, believes the Epistle to Eahfrith is actually addressed to Aldfrith on the occasion of his return from Ireland some time before he became king in 685. Cook calls "Eahfrith" an "unaccountable spelling for 'Ealdfrith'." A later communication from Aldhelm to Aldfrith, the *Epistle to Acircius*, was written during Aldfrith's reign at Bamburgh.

40 George F. Browne, *St. Aldhelm* (London, 1903), p. 263.

41 For the text of the letter, see *Patrologiae cursus completus*, Series Latina, ed. J. P. Migne (Paris, 1863), LXXXIX, cols. 92–95.

42 See Chapter I, n. 3 above, for references about Gaulish learning in the fourth and fifth centuries. On Gaulish monastic organization and its influence on the Irish, see Ryan, *Irish Monastic-*

*ism*, pp. 53–56, 94–95. The famous passage in the Leyden Glossary telling of the flight to Ireland of Gaulish refugees is given in Kenney, *Sources*, I, 142. On the routes used by such refugees, see Archibald A. Lewis, "Le commerce et la navigation sur les côtes atlantiques de la Gaule du Vᵉ au VIIIᵉ siècle," *Le Moyen Age*, LVIII (1952), 247–98; also H. O'Neill Hencken, *The Archaeology of Cornwall and Scilly* (London, 1932), p. 172. The Irish would repay this debt during the ninth and tenth centuries when their own scholars sought sanctuary on the Continent from Scandinavian plunderers.

43 Ryan, *Irish Monasticism*, p. 378. For strong proof of Irish concentration on Biblical exegesis in the seventh and eighth centuries see Bernhard Bischoff, "Wendepunkte in der Geschichte der lateinischen Exegese im Frühmittelalter," *Sacris Erudiri*, VI (1954), 189–281.

44 Ryan, *Irish Monasticism*, pp. 379–80. On the education and duties of the *ollam* see O'Curry, *Lectures on the Manuscript Materials*, pp. 204, 240–41. Aldfrith in his poem (page 29, above) refers to the "historians recording truth," a reference to one of the chief functions of the *ollam*, that of keeping accurate records of the growth and development of individual clans and royal houses. On *sui littre*, see *Contributions to a Dictionary of the Irish Language*, S, ed. E. G. Quin, Royal Irish Academy (Dublin, 1953), col. 412, l. 37.

45 *Vit. Sanct. Hib.*, ed. Plummer, I, 35.

46 *Ibid.*, II, 22. See also Ryan, *Irish Monasticism*, p. 378, n. 6.

47 Roger, *L'Enseignement des lettres classiques*, pp. 228–29.

48 ". . . il y a une région de l'ancien monde où la tradition des lettres latines, des lettres grecques, s'est conservée, où des multitudes de jeunes Chrétiens entourent des maîtres qui leur enseignent à comprendre Homère et Virgile; et cette région, c'est l'Irlande." — Barthélemy Hauréau, *Singularités Historiques et Littéraires* (Paris, 1861), p. 1.

49 Ryan, *Irish Monasticism*, pp. 371–73. See also Bede, *H. E.* III, 13.

50 Mario Esposito, "Notes on Latin Learning and Literature in Medieval Ireland," *Hermathena*, XX (1930), 236 *et seq.* Also the same author with Louis Gougaud, "Notes on the Latin Writers of Mediaeval Ireland," *Irish Theological Quarterly*, IV (1909), 57–65, 181–85; Eoin MacNeill, "Beginnings of Latin Culture in Ireland," *Studies*, XX (1931), 39–48, 449–60.

51 John Healy, "St. Cummain the Tall, Bishop of Clonfert," *Irish Ecclesiastical Record*, 3rd Series, VII (1886), 1–16.

52 William Reeves, "On Augustin, an Irish Writer of the Seventh

Century," *Proceedings of the Royal Irish Academy,* VII (1861), 514–22.

53  Max Manitius, *Geschichte der Lateinischen Literatur des Mittelalters* (Munich, 1911), I, 10.

54  Adamnan's non-intellectual activities included an expedition to find lumber for the monastery and a trip to Bamburgh to intervene with his friend, King Aldfrith, on behalf of Irishmen taken prisoner and carried back to Northumbria after Ecgfrith's ill-fated Irish raid of 684.

55  Brüning, in *Zeitschrift für Celtische Philologie,* XI (1917), 241: "Neben diesen biblischen Anklängen begegnen in der Lebensbeschreibung Columbas auch klassische Reminiszenzen, die uns wieder den gelehrten Verfasser zeigen. Besonders Vergil war im Mittelalter sehr beliebt, und auch Adamnan ist in seiner Sprache von ihm beeinflusst."

56  *Ibid.,* p. 244: "All diese Anklänge sind sicher zum grossen Teil aus dem Gedächtnis niedergeschrieben, und die Quelle lässt sich nur mit Wahrscheinlichkeit vermuten. Sie zeigen vor allem Adamnans Belesenheit und Bekanntschaft mit der römischen Literatur."

57  Notable among this group are Clement the Irishman (fl. 826), who succeeded Alcuin as master of the palace school at Aachen; Dungal, author of a treastise (811) on a recent eclipse; and Dicuil, astronomer and geographer (fl. 814–825), who wrote *De Mensura Orbis Terrae.* See William Turner, "Irish Teachers in the Carolingian Revival," *Catholic University Bulletin,* XIII (1907), 386–94.

58  E. K. Rand, "A *Vade Mecum* of Liberal Culture in a Manuscript of Fleury," *Philological Quarterly,* I (1922), 274.

59  Kenney, *Sources,* I, 559–60.

60  James M. Clark, *The Abbey of St. Gall as a Centre of Literature and Art* (Cambridge, 1926), pp. 298–99.

61  Walther Schultze, "Die Bedeutung der iroschottischen Mönche für die Erhaltung und Fortpflanzung der mittelalterlichen Wissenschaft," *Centralblatt für Bibliothekswesen,* VI (1889), 193–94: "Es wurden denn in der That in Irland auch die classischen Autoren abgeschrieben, zum Theil mit irischen Glossen versehen: derartige Handschriften besitzen wir z. B. von Horaz und Priscian. In den Klöstern wurden Ovid und Virgil gelesen. Manche der irischen Autoren besitzen classische Bildung." See also p. 186.

62  See Max Manitius, *Handschriften Antiker Autoren in Mittelalterlichen Bibliothekskatalogen* (Leipzig, 1935), *passim,* for location of MSS of Donatus and Servius the grammarians, Plautus, Ter-

ence, Cicero, and Sallust at Irish Continental centers including Reichenau, St. Gall, and Bobbio. St. Columbanus, whose labors on the Continent in the sixth century were similar to those of Columba of Iona, "feared lest, ensnared by the lusts of the world, he should in vain have spent so much labor on grammar, rhetoric, geometry and Holy Scripture." See also *Life of St. Columban by the Monk, Jonas,* ed. and trans. Dana C. Munro (Philadelphia, 1897), p. 3.

63 J. D. A. Ogilvy, *Books Known to Anglo-Latin Writers from Aldhelm to Alcuin* (Cambridge, Mass., 1936), pp. 1, 13–20, 49–55.

64 Alexander Souter, "The Sources of Sedulius Scottus' *Collectaneum* on the Epistles of St. Paul," *Journal of Theological Studies,* XVIII (1917), 184.

65 *H. E.,* V, 15. "Furthermore, Adamnan presented this book to king Aldfrid, and by his liberality it was handed on to inferior persons to read."—*Baedae Opera historica,* trans. King, II, 285.

66 In *H. E.,* IV, 26, Bede writes: " . . . he [Aldfrith] did nobly recover the ruined estate of the kingdom, though the bounds thereof were now more narrow."—*Baedae Opera historica,* trans. King, II, 165. See also Cook, in *Transactions of the Connecticut Society of Arts and Sciences,* XXV, 287–88, 306–7.

CHAPTER IV

1 Altogether, there are six canticles, twelve metrical hymns, sixty-nine collects for use at Canonical hours, seventeen collects for special persons and occasions, twenty anthems and versicles, the Creed and the Pater Noster in its folios. The Antiphonary is similar to service-books carried to the Continent by Bangor-trained St. Columbanus (d. 615). A comparison of the rule established by Columbanus for monasteries at Bobbio and Luxeuil with certain items in the Antiphonary points up the influence of this humble document and others like it outside Ireland.— Kenney, *Sources,* I, 198. For the text of the Rule, see *Patrologiae cursus completus,* Series Latina, ed. J. P. Migne (Paris, 1863), LXXX, cols. 209–24. The rules for the distribution of the Psalter throughout the religious year found in the Antiphonary are identical with those given in the Rule of Columbanus, which also copied the peculiar arrangement of night hours prescribed by the Antiphonary. This scheme, calling for the presence of the monks at three additional services after Vespers (*Ad Initium Noctis, Ad Nocturnum,* and *Ad Matutinam*), was probably followed by the Lindisfarne *familia.* It demanded rising at the hours of nine, twelve, and three in the hours of darkness, to hear the Psalms read. See *The Antiphonary of Bangor,* ed. War-

ren, I, *passim.* See also, William Reeves, "The *Antiphonary of Bangor,*" *Ulster Journal of Archaeology,* I (1853), 168–79; W. C. Bishop, "A Service Book of the Seventh Century," *Church Quarterly Review,* XXXVII (1894), 337–63; Robert Culhane, "The Bangor Hymn to Christ the King," *Irish Ecclesiastical Record,* 5th Series, LXXIV (1950), 207–19.

2 E. A. Lowe, "Handwriting," in *The Legacy of the Middle Ages,* eds. Charles G. Crump and E. F. Jacob (Oxford, 1926), p. 198. For the value of paleography to studies of this type, see Ludwig Bieler, "Palaeography and Spiritual Tradition," *Studies,* XXIX (1940), 269–80. Also N. Denholm-Young, *Handwriting in England and Wales* (Cardiff, 1954), pp. 1–8; François Masai, "La Paléographie Gréco-Latine, Ses Tâches, Ses Méthodes," *Scriptorium,* X (1956), 281–302.

3 Adamnan, *Life of St. Columba,* ed. Reeves, p. 3.

4 *Ibid.,* p. 97.

5 *Ibid.,* p. 20.

6 Ryan, *Irish Monasticism,* pp. 380–381.

7 *Ven. Baedae Hist. eccl.,* ed. Plummer, I, xx.

8 See *Thesaurus Palaeohibernicus,* eds. Stokes and Strachan, II, xx, xxi, xxii, for these and other examples of Irish marginalia taken from the St. Gall Priscian prepared in Ireland "in the first half of the ninth century, and brought by wandering Irishmen to the Continent." See also Charles Plummer, "On the Colophons and Marginalia of Irish Scribes," *Proceedings of the British Academy,* XII (1926), 11–44.

9 A defense of these blunders on the ground that the copyists worked under pressure and in haste is ill-founded. No evidence exists to suggest that the Irish copyist was allotted a daily quota of lines or folios to complete.

10 However, compare first-century wall inscriptions (Fig. 1, A) with Pompeian waxen tablets (Thompson, *Handbook,* p. 208).

11 For a facsimile of this MS, see Heinrich Fichtenau, *Mensch und Schrift im Mittelalter* (Vienna, 1946), Plate II.

12 Among those taking part in the controversy have been Wolfgang Keller, "Angelsächsische Schrift," *Reallexikon der Germanischen Altertumskunde,* ed. Johannes Hoops (Strassburg, 1911), I, 98–103. Also Cesare Paoli, *Programma scolastico di paleografia latina e di diplomatica* (Florence, 1888), pp. 18–19.

13 Schiaparelli, in *Archivio storico Italiano,* LXXIV (1916), Pt. II, 3–126. See also *Codices,* ed. Lowe, II, xii. Lowe writes of the Irish semi-uncial: " . . . its origins are shrouded in obscurity. Palaeographers agree, however, that it is based, in the main, on half-uncial, of which it is a modification." See Thompson,

*Handbook,* pp. 236–37. An opinion is expressed in *Lexikon des gesamten Buchwesens,* eds. Karl Löffler and Joachim Kirchner (Leipzig, 1935), I, 59, that the Continental uncial played a more important part in the development of Insular writing than has generally been acknowledged.

14 Thompson, *Handbook,* p. 239, believes that the ornamental round hand, "remarkable both for its solidity and its graceful outlines" is a natural complement to the interlaced designs, the "skillful drawing" and "brilliant colouring" of Gospel MSS like the Book of Kells, which he assigns to the seventh century.

15 *Ibid.,* pp. 241, 242. See lines from the *Book of Armagh.* The pointed hand apparently developed after the semi-uncial round hand.

16 Wolfgang Keller, "Angelsächsische Palaeographie," *Palaestra,* XLIII (1906), 18. Franz Steffens, *Lateinische Paläographie* (Trier, 1909), xiv: "Mit der Zeit nahm aber die römische Halbunciale in Irland gewisse eigentümliche Formen an, und so enstand die nationale irische Schrift." See also, Bertold Bretholz, *Lateinische Paläographie* (Leipzig, 1926), p. 60.

17 Thompson, *Handbook,* pp. 248–51.

18 *Dictionnaire d'Archéologie Chrétienne et de Liturgie,* ed. Fernand Cabrol (Paris, 1910), II, Part I, cols. 183–91.

19 See my Fig. 2, l. 1, "Cantemus dño."

20 Fig. 2, l. 4 from bottom, "glorificata."

21 Fig. 2, l. 1, "Cantemus."

22 Fig. 2, l. 9, "in mare."

23 Fig. 2, l. 1, "gloriosae."

24 Ruling lines can be seen in ll. 7–11 of Fig. 2.

25 See Fig. 2, margin at left and right of last four lines.

26 These include signs for *bene, benedicite, autem, pro passim, per, nostro,* and *nostrum.*

27 Ludwig Traube, "Perrona Scottorum: ein Beitrag zur Überlieferungsgeschichte und zur Palaeographie des Mittelalters," *Vorlesungen und Abhandlungen von Ludwig Traube,* ed. Franz Boll (Munich, 1920), III, 95–100. See Schiaparelli in *Archivio storico italiano,* LXXIV, Pt. II, 21; also Ludwig Bieler, "Insular Palaeography: Present State and Problems," *Scriptorium,* III (1949), 267–94.

28 Lindsay, *Early Irish Minuscule,* and Adriano Cappelli, *Lexicon Abbreviaturarum* (Milan, 1949). Lindsay pointed to the presence of similar abbreviation signs in most Irish and English MSS.

29 Leslie W. Jones, "Pricking Systems in N. Y. Mss.," *Miscellanea Giovanni Mercati* (Vatican City, 1946), VI, 80–92. Lowe, *Codices,* II, vi, writes: "If a manuscript is written in non-Insular script

but is pricked in the Insular manner we must surmise Insular origin or influence. Interesting cases in point are the *Codex Amiatinus* . . . and the *Stonyhurst Gospel,* all in beautiful uncial characters which some writers have thought the work of Italian scribes—a theory discredited by the prickings, if nothing else."

30  *Codices,* ed. Lowe, II, viii.

31  *Ibid.,* p. vi.

32  *Ibid.,* p. vii. Lowe notes that quinions were common in Oriental MSS and suggests that the Irish may have first received the idea from them. "The Irish word for book, I am informed, may be a corruption of quinion, and the Anglo-Saxon *cine* seems to be borrowed from the Irish."

33  *Ibid.,* p. vii.

34  E. A. Lowe, "The Oldest Omission Signs in Latin Mss," *Miscellanea Giovanni Mercati,* VI, 76. Commenting on this practice, Lowe writes: "It doubtless dates back to the seventh century. For we find this pair of symbols in the restoration of the book of Kings in the famous Plautus palimpsest in the portion where the restoring hand is Irish majuscule of the seventh century . . . if not earlier. This method was also known in England, for we find it in the Lindisfarne Gospels written about A.D. 700. But whereas English scribes in the homeland as well as on the Continent make constant use of *d* and *h* . . . Irish scribes on the whole use *signes de renvoi,* such as obeloi, crosses, asterisks, and similar combinations of lines and dots."

35  *Codices,* ed. Lowe, II, viii. Lowe comments: "This ignorance or disregard of ancient Latin practice proves how unaffected Insular scribes were by the tradition prevailing on the Continent."

36  Note particularly ll. 1, 5, and 12, Fig. 2, for examples of the triangle-topped shaft.

37  *Codices,* ed. Lowe, II, xii. Lowe suggests that the reader compare the Book of Kells with the Lindisfarne Gospels, or the Book of Mulling with the Moore Bede to see this difference.

38  *Ibid.* To see these criteria utilized by an expert paleographer, the reader should check such MS descriptions as the following in *Codices,* ed. Lowe, II: No. 147, *Durham Cathedral Library* A. II. 10, "written presumably in Northumbria, by a scribe trained in the pure Irish tradition"; No. 149, *Durham Cathedral Library* A. II. 17, Insular majuscule of the seventh or eighth century, "written probably in Northumbria, in a great centre of calligraphy in the direct line of Irish tradition, or else in Ireland itself"; No. 125, *Cambridge, Corpus Christi College* 197, Insular majuscule of the eighth century, probably written in Northumbria "certainly in an important English centre familiar

with Irish calligraphy"; No. 133, *Cambridge, Trinity College* B. 10. 5, Insular minuscule of the eighth century, with coarse and rough vellum and an "elaborate system of points employed as reference-signs" recalling Irish habits, "written in England probably by an Irish scribe"; No. 184, *Cotton Cleopatra* A. III*, Anglo-Saxon minuscule of the eighth century, "written in England, probably in the North, in a centre with Irish traditions." Also items 132, 157, 148b, 179, 218, 256, 273, Dublin, *Trinity College* 57 (A. IV. 5) The Book of Durrow, Gospels written in Northumbria "by a hand trained in the Irish manner, and copied from an exemplar in the hand of St. Columba, the founder of Durrow, to judge by the subscriptions on fol. 12v."

39  See Blanche B. Boyer, "Insular Contribution to Medieval Literary Tradition on the Continent," *Classical Philology,* XLII (1947), 209–22 and *ibid.,* XLIII (1948), 31–39. Surveying the extant manuscripts written by Insular copyists, Miss Boyer finds 550 Latin MSS of the eighth to tenth centuries of which 400 are wholly Insular, with the remaining 150 divided into three classes of approximately 50 each, all Insular "in part and in decreasing degree, on the basis of (1) mixture; (2) corrections, glosses, and marginal notes; (3) influence in writing practices."

40  See Chapter I, nn. 41, 42, 43, 44, above.

41  Adamnan, *Life of St. Columba,* ed. Reeves, p. 35.

42  *Ibid.,* pp. 86–87.

43  *Ibid.,* p. 90.

44  More scribal obits are recorded for Bangor than for any other Irish monastery in the eighth century. "The explanation for Bangor's failure to develop in the ninth century and her collapse in the tenth may be found . . . in the narrow limitations of her financial resources."—Kathleen Hughes, "The Distribution of Irish Scriptoria and Centres of Learning from 730 to 1111," in *Studies in the Early British Church,* ed. Chadwick, p. 260.

CHAPTER V

1  Adamnan, *Life of St. Columba,* ed. Reeves, pp. 101–2 of the translation. For the Latin text of the subscription, see *ibid.,* p. 218.

2  *Ibid.,* pp. xix–xxxi; also Mario Esposito, "Hiberno-Latin Manuscripts in the Libraries of Switzerland," *Proceedings of the Royal Irish Academy,* XXVIII (1910), C, 71–72. See also Heinrich Boos, *Verzeichnis der Inkunabeln und Handschriften der Schaffhauser Stadtbibliothek* (Schaffhausen, 1903), p. 67.

3  *Codices,* ed. Lowe, VII, 45.

4  *Ibid.*

5  *Ibid.*

6 *Ibid.* Lowe notes that Dorbene's *e* often rises above the head-
line, that the shoulder of his *r* bends very low, and that *y* has
two forms, "both going below the line and one being typically
Irish with both branches curving to the right." Also the "oblique
of *z* thrusts far below the line."

7 *Ibid.* Lowe finds that  **ƕ** = *autem*;  **ƀ** = *bene*;  Ɔ = *con*; Ǝ ,
**Ħ, ÷** = *eius, enim,* and *est,* among others.

8 *Ibid.*

9 *Ibid.* See also Chap. IV, n. 37, above.

10 Lindsay, *Early Irish Minuscule,* pp. 1–2. His evidence comes from
f. 108 of the manuscript where the first column, with the exception of the first and last lines, is written wholly in a smaller
script. Apparently Dorbene had left a blank space here in which
he meant to refer to an earlier life of Columba, *De virtutibus
Sancti Columbae,* written by Cuimine, seventh abbot of Iona.
But when he came to fill this gap, Dorbene found that he had
miscalculated the space required, and consequently was forced
to reduce the size of his script.

11 According to Hugh J. Lawlor, in *Proceedings of the Roy. Ir.
Acad.,* XXXIII, C, 241–44.

12 William Betham, *Irish Antiquarian Researches* (Dublin, 1827),
pp. 110–11.

13 O'Curry, *Lectures on the Manuscript Materials,* p. 332. See Mario
Esposito's notes on the Cathach, "The So-called Psalter of St.
Columba," *Notes and Queries,* XI (1915), 253–54, 466–68. See
also, Duncan M. Maclennan, "The Cathach of Colum-cille,"
*Transactions of the Gaelic Society of Inverness,* XXXV (1939),
2–25. Lowe, *Codices,* II, 41, states that a sixth-century date for
the Cathach is paleographically possible. Hugh J. Lawlor, in
*Proceedings of the Roy. Ir. Acad.,* XXXIII, C, 292–93, quotes
extracts from a life of Columba prepared by Manus O'Donnell
in 1532 where the episode of the illegal copying appears.

14 *Codices,* ed. Lowe, II, 41.

15 *Ibid.* See my Fig. 4 (facsimile of folio 52r), lines 6–11 from
bottom, both margins, for these prickings.

16 *Codices,* ed. Lowe, II, 41.

17 Hugh J. Lawlor, in *Proceedings of the Roy. Ir. Acad.,* XXXIII, C,
248–50.

18 *Ibid.,* p. 326.

19 See *Evangeliorum Quattuor: Codex Cenannensis.*

20 Adamnan, *Life of St. Columba,* ed. Reeves, pp. li–lii.

21 See Albert M. Friend, Jr., "The Canon Tables of the *Book of
Kells,*" *Medieval Studies in Memory of A. Kingsley Porter,* ed.

W. R. Koehler (Cambridge, 1939), II, 611–66. Friend advances
the dates 795–806 for composition of the Book of Kells.
22 *Annals of Ulster,* ed. Hennessy, I, 519. See Aubrey Gwynn,
"Some Notes on the History of the *Book of Kells,*" *Irish Historical
Studies,* IX (1954–55), 131–61.
23 Arthur P. Laurie, *The Materials of the Painter's Craft* (London,
1910), p. 247. See R. Powell, "The *Book of Kells,* the *Book of
Durrow*: Comments on the Vellum, the Make-up and Other
Aspects," *Scriptorium,* X (1956), 3–21.
24 OE. *gabolrind* ("compass") is one of the authentic loan words
from Irish given by Förster in *Keltisches Wortgut im Englischen,*
p. 45.
25 Luce, in *Hermathena,* LXXIX, 72.
26 See *Evangeliorum Quattuor: Codex Lindisfarnensis.* For a letter-
press edition, see *The Lindisfarne and Rushworth Gospels,* Surtees Society, Vols. XXVIII (1854), XXXIX (1861), XLIII
(1863), XLVIII (1865), (Durham).
27 Kenney, *Sources,* I, 651. R. A. S. Macalister, "The Colophon
in the *Lindisfarne Gospels,*" in *Essays and Studies Presented to
William Ridgeway,* ed. Edmund C. Quiggin (Cambridge, 1913),
299–305, claims the colophon to be spurious. According to his
theory the Lindisfarne Gospels was done in Ireland and stolen
by Anglo-Saxons who scribbled the glosses and other notes and
asserted that Saxons wrote it! "If we say that it was written
about 830 A.D., glossed about 930, and that it changed hands
some time between 840 and 890, we shall do no violence to
historic possibility. . . . "
28 On Ethilwald, see the note in *Ven. Baedae Hist. eccl.,* ed. Plummer, II, 297–98. A stone cross erected at Lindisfarne by Ethilwald's order and carrying his name "shared the wanderings of
St. Cuthbert's body till it reposed at Durham." The glosses for
both the Lindisfarne Gospels and the Durham Ritual may have
been written by Aldred. See Neil R. Ker, "Aldred the Scribe,"
*Essays and Studies,* XXVIII (1942), 7–12. For possible Irish
influence on spelling in the Lindisfarne Gospels, see Alan S. C.
Ross, *Studies in the Accidence of the Lindisfarne Gospels* (Leeds,
1937), pp. 161–62.
29 Luce, in *Hermathena,* LXXIX, 63. Comparing the Lindisfarne Gospels, 124r, and the Book of Kells, 176v and 177r, Luce
points out that the Kells scribe allows two pages for a passage
contained in one page in the Lindisfarne MS.
30 *Codices,* ed. Lowe, II, 20.
31 Luce, in *Hermathena,* LXXIX, 73–74. Compare the Lindisfarne
Gospels, 124r and the Book of Kells, 176v and 177r.

32 Brown, *Arts in Early England,* V, 346: " . . . small capitals are
used to mark—not the chapters and verses—but certain divisions
of the text numbered in brown ink and in red at the side of
each of the two columns of writing on the page. The loops of
these small capitals are filled in with flat tints of yellow and
of blue and the dots . . . are red." Luce, in *Hermathena,*
LXXIX, 72, states that the Book of Kells has more color and
a wider range of colors than the Lindisfarne Gospels. He also
writes, p. 62, that the Lindisfarne Gospels in contrast to the
Book of Kells is "plain . . . in that it economizes colour and
other ornament, keeps close to common standards, and rarely
rises to the heights. It is rigid in that it keeps to plan; its ornament is often stiff and repetitive and gives little play to the
imagination." For a "minute study of pigments employed by
insular illuminations, Irish and Anglo-Saxon, based chiefly on the
*Book of Lindisfarne,*" see Arthur P. Laurie, *The Pigments and
Mediums of the Old Masters* (London, 1914).

33 Luce, in *Hermathena,* LXXX, 12–13, believes this discrepancy
in the number of pages given to the Canon Tables in the two
books is important for an understanding of the difference in
tone and purpose that marks them. The Canon Tables, a type
of concordance, were meant for *use* in the Lindisfarne Gospels
and for *symbolic importance* in the Book of Kells. Eadfrith
"devotes to the contents of the Tables the care and precision
of a guide-book, and expands where *Kells* compresses." To Luce,
this is corroboration for his thesis that the Lindisfarne Gospels
has a "hieratic flavor." Having been commissioned by a bishop,
it is a "priest's book," rather than a "people's book" as is the
Book of Kells.

34 Herbert, *Illuminated Manuscripts,* pp. 74–75.

35 However, see Masai's argument in favor of a Northumbrian
origin for Insular illumination techniques in his *Essai sur les
origines de la miniature dite Irlandaise.* See Ludwig Bieler's
review of this provocative book in *Speculum,* XXIII (1948),
495–502; also the unsigned review in *English Historical Review,*
LXIII (1948), 395–96.

36 David Diringer, *The Hand-Produced Book* (New York, 1953),
p. 505.

37 Figure portraiture was the weakest aspect of Insular illumination. See John O. Westwood, *Palaeographia Sacra Pictoria*
(London, 1843–45), the Gospels of St. Chad, folio 109v. In this
Gospel codex, prepared at about the same time as the Lindisfarne Gospels in a Welsh monastery where Irish influence was
strong, we see the figure of St. Luke done in the Irish style.

Herbert, *Illuminated Manuscripts,* p. 76, describes it: "The drawing of the figure touches the limit of grotesque hideousness: the body composed of a series of bulging curves; the hair divided into neatly fitting segments and coloured red, yellow, and purple; the huge head, with its staring eyes and impossible nose—all combine to form a *reductio ad absurdum* of the Irish manner."

CHAPTER VI

1 See Chapter I, n. 66, above.

2 Adamnan, *Life of St. Columba,* ed. Reeves, pp. 33, 96. Adoration of the Cross began with Constantine's conversion and victory over Maxentius in 312.

3 *Ibid.,* pp. 48, 56, 57, for example. Allusions to Columba's ability to use the sign of the cross in highly efficacious ways—from blessing milk pails and tools to repelling water monsters—are scattered through Adamnan's book. Max Förster notes one occurrence of OE *cros* in a tenth-century charter where the word could quite possibly be a borrowing from the Scandinavian.— *Keltisches Wortgut im Englischen,* pp. 28–36. On Anglo-Saxon uses of the cross see Stevens, *Cross in Life and Lit. of Anglo-Saxons.* Bede tells that St. Cuthbert, at least once, extended himself in the form of a cross (cross-vigil) to pray (*H. E.* IV, 29). According to another source, he did so again on seeing Aidan's soul taken to heaven. Alcuin, too, had resorted to what the Irish termed *crosfigil.—Ven. Baedae Hist. eccl.,* ed. Plummer, II, 269–70. For the Irish practice of *crosfigil* in the eighth century, see Edward J. Gwynn and W. J. Purton, "The Monastery of Tallaght," *Proceedings of the Royal Irish Academy,* XXIX (1911-12), C, 137–38. Before his death in 687, Cuthbert ordered a stone cross made, portions of which may have accompanied his coffin on its extended journey through Northumbria and Durham after 875. For Old English literature of the cross, see *The Homilies of Aelfric,* ed. and trans. B. Thorpe, Aelfric Society (London, 1846), II, 303–7; *History of the Holy Rood-Tree,* ed. Arthur S. Napier, Early English Text Society, (London, 1894).

4 Stevens, *Cross in Life and Lit. of Anglo-Saxons,* pp. 30–37, points out uses of the cross and its sign among Anglo-Saxons as a protective shield, an oath on documents, preceding inscriptions on stone slabs and crosses, and on inscribed rings and jewels. It had been used also on coins as early as 665. See also Albert Keiser, *The Influence of Christianity on the Vocabulary of Old English Poetry* (Urbana, 1919), pp. 79–81.

5 Hodgkin, *History of the Anglo-Saxons,* I, 363–64.

6 Joseph Strzygowski, *Origin of Christian Church Art* (Oxford, 1923), p. 230.

7 Masai, *Essai sur les origines de la miniature dite Irlandaise,* p. 36.

8 Henry, *Irish Art in the Early Christian Period,* p. 72.

9 Brown, *Arts in Early England,* VI, Pt. II, 163–64.

10 Alfred W. Clapham, "Notes on the Origins of Hiberno-Saxon Art," *Antiquity,* VIII (1934), 56–57.

11 *Ibid.,* p. 57.

12 Macalister, *Archaeology of Ireland,* p. 97. Morey, *Mediaeval Art,* pp. 182–83.

13 See folios 29r, 33r, 34r, 130r, and 188r in the Book of Kells.— J. Romilly Allen, *Celtic Art in Pagan and Christian Times,* 2nd ed. rev. (London, 1912), p. 287; J. Romilly Allen, *The Early Christian Monuments of Scotland* (Edinburgh, 1903), Pt. I, pp. 374–75.

14 Morey, *Mediaeval Art,* p. 184, believes the interlace motif could have been copied from Roman mosaic pavement in Britain. See my Fig. 7, particularly A, B, C, D, E, H, and J, for examples of interlace on fragments of crosses at Lindisfarne.

15 Morey, *Mediaeval Art,* p. 184, notes that the Irish interlace is distinguished by "excessive complication" containing "no loose" ends and no plain loops.

16 In his analysis of the *Book of Durrow,* Thomas D. Kendrick, *Anglo-Saxon Art to A.D. 900* (London, 1938), pp. 98–99, writes: the "ornamental scheme of the Durrow pages is nothing more nor less than a developed barbaric version of the Roman decorative schemes so well established by our late mosaic pavements of the west country type."

17 Morey, *Mediaeval Art,* p. 184, believes the key pattern to have been picked up from Latin art by Celtic artists on the Continent and transmitted by them to Ireland. In the process of transmission the rectangular verticals and horizontals of the Greco-Roman changed to diagonals. See Fig. 7, particularly C, F, H and K, for examples of key motif on fragments of crosses at Lindisfarne.—Allen, *Early Christian Monuments,* Pt. I, pp. 331–63. See also *Recent Archaeological Excavations in Britain,* ed. Robert L. Bruce-Mitford (London, 1956), Plates XVIIb and XVIIIa, for mosaic floor with Greek key border in Roman villa, Lullingstone, Kent.

18 Bernhard Salin, *Die Altgermanische Thierornamentik* (Stockholm, 1904), pp. 322–49. See also David T. Rice, *English Art 871–1100* (Oxford, 1952), pp. 125–26.

19 See folios 3r, 130r, and 188r of the Book of Kells. See Fig. 9

(Monk's Stone at Tynemouth), particularly A, for combination of animal figures and interlace motif.

20 See Fig. 9 (Monk's Stone at Tynemouth), particularly B, for leaf-and-vine motif with animal figures interspersed.

21 Eric H. Sexton, *A Descriptive and Bibliographical List of Irish Figure Sculptures* (Portland, 1946), pp. 4–6, restates Brown's theory that originally, plain crosses were set up principally as memorials in the fifth or sixth centuries by Celtic missionaries. See also Jackson, *Lang. and Hist. in Early Britain*, pp. 165–66. See *Sculptured Stones of Scotland*, ed. J. Stuart, II, 15. Designs for the crosses may have been worked out with ropes or twigs and then reproduced in stone.

22 *Sculptured Stones of Scotland*, ed. Stuart, II, 20. See also Mac-alister, *Corpus inscriptionum insularum Celticarum*, I, 310, in which the author describes how a sixth-century stone in Wales was "barbarously trimmed square, some time before 1847 to fit into the wall of the church chancel, where it is now to be seen."

23 See Fritz Saxl, "The Ruthwell Cross," *Journal of the Warburg and Courtauld Institutes*, VI (1943), 1–19, for excellent photographs of the Ruthwell Cross. The article is reprinted in his *England and the Mediterranean Tradition* (London, 1945).

24 *The Dream of the Rood*, eds. Bruce Dickins and Alan S. C. Ross, 2nd ed. (London, 1945), pp. 4–5. See also Ross, "The Linguistic Evidence for the Date of the Ruthwell Cross," *Modern Language Review*, XXVIII (1933), 146. The dialect is Northumbrian and "is probably very similar to that represented in the *Lindisfarne Gospels*."

25 William R. Lethaby, "Is Ruthwell Cross an Anglo-Celtic Work?" *Archaeological Journal*, LXX (1913), 145–61.

26 Hodgkin, *History of the Anglo-Saxons*, I, 362.

27 Brown, *Arts in Early England*, V, 21–22. See also *The Anglo-Saxon Minor Poems*, ed. Dobbie, p. cxxii: "The evidence of both sculpture and language . . . points to some time in the first half of the eighth century as the most probable date for the Ruthwell Cross and its inscription."

28 Brown, *Arts in Early England*, V, 314. Hodgkin, *History of the Anglo-Saxons*, I, 301, appraises Whitby as a Roman victory decisive yet somewhat limited "because, strictly speaking, it only applied to one kingdom; because it only related to two diversities of custom; because it allowed other Celtic peculiarities to continue; and because it did not put an end to jealousies and ill feelings between the two schools within the Church." See also Chapter III, n. 1, above.

29 Hodgkin, *History of the Anglo-Saxons*, I, 363–64, writes that

Anglian makers of the Bewcastle Cross took the idea of the
tall cross from the Celts and that the Roman letters on its face
are written in an Irish style. See also Porter, *Crosses and Culture
of Ireland,* pp. 100–101. He thinks that the lower panel on the
left face of the Bewcastle Cross portrays Columba of Iona and
a dove. The book in the panel might well be the Columba
Cathach described in Chapter V, above, and what has been
taken for a falcon's perch might be a crozier. Porter writes:
"If this identification be correct, the Bewcastle Cross preserves
for us the earliest extant iconography of the great Irish saint."
Porter, pp. 97–99, points also to the fact that despite Wilfrid's
and Benedict Biscop's success in importing Roman artistic and
architectural forms, the latter's church at Monkwearmouth must
have had a purely Celtic plan and the "front elevation seems
also Irish."

30  Meyer Schapiro, "The Religious Meaning of the Ruthwell Cross,"
    *Art Bulletin,* XXVI (1944), 232.

31  See Fig. 10, above. See Henry G. Leach, "Tynwald Day on the
    Isle of Man," *The American Scandinavian Review,* XLIII (1955),
    125–36 for Norwegian epic combat motifs, involving chiefly Odin
    and Sigurd the Volsung, that were applied to Manx crosses.
    The Norwegians apparently adopted the Manx cross for their
    tombstones and decorated it with motifs from their pagan past.

32  James Carney, *Studies in Irish Literature and History* (Dublin,
    1955), pp. 121–23; also *Vit. Sanct. Hib.,* ed. Plummer, I, cxxxix.

33  Porter, *Crosses and Culture of Ireland,* pp. 86–87, believes that
    the Saints Paul and Anthony motif originated in Egypt, that it
    "was first represented in Egypt in some lost prototype, and
    that the iconography was thence carried to Ireland and no doubt
    also to Northumbria." He also holds that the John the Baptist
    motif in relief on both the Bewcastle and Ruthwell Crosses
    came originally from Egypt. In *De locis sanctis,* Adamnan
    recorded the Gallic Bishop Arculf's vivid eye-witness description
    of the site on the river Jordan where John had baptized Christ.
    Arculf tells of the "wooden cross of great size" fixed on the
    site, "close to which the water comes up to the neck of the
    tallest man."—*Pilgrimage of Arculfus,* trans. Macpherson, p. 37.
    As noted in Chapter III, above, Adamnan had carried *De locis
    sanctis* from Iona to Northumbria as a gift for King Aldfrith.
    See also *Adamnan's "De locis sanctis,"* ed. Denis Meehan (Dub-
    lin, 1958).

34  Robin Flower, "Irish High Crosses," *Journal of the Warburg and
    Courtauld Institutes,* XVII (1954), 89.

35  *Vit. Sanct. Hib.,* ed. Plummer, I, cxliii–cxlvi. Animals helpful

and friendly to the Irish saints included stags, otters, sea birds, foxes, and swans. See Sister Mary Donatus, *Beasts and Birds in the Lives of the Early Irish Saints* (Philadelphia, 1934). Aldhelm and Cuthbert, whose Irish affiliations have been touched on in earlier chapters, were on good terms with animals. See the episode of the "apologetic crows" in *Two Lives of St. Cuthbert*, ed. and trans. Bertram Colgrave (Cambridge, 1940), pp. 222–25. Here the "friendly animal" motif may appear in an English setting as an adaptation from Irish hagiography.

36  Schapiro, in *Art Bulletin*, XXVI, 243–45.

37  See Charles W. Kennedy, *The Earliest English Poetry* (New York, 1943), pp. 261–62. He points out that the diction of the poem is mainly Cynewulfian, that Cynewulf "had written and signed another poem on the Cross," and that the "somewhat extended passage at the end of the *Dream* is remarkably similar in substance and tone to the personal passages which conclude the *Christ* and *Elene*." George K. Anderson, *The Literature of the Anglo-Saxons* (Princeton, 1949), p. 141: "Probably it was written, if not by Cynewulf, at least by a poet of Cynewulfian persuasion. . . . " See, however, *The Vercelli Book*, ed. Krapp, p. xl.

38  *The Vercelli Book*, ed. Krapp, pp. 100–101.

39  Carleton F. Brown, "Irish-Latin Influence in Cynewulfian Texts," *Englische Studien*, XL (1909), 1–29, argues the case for an Irish source for Cynewulf's writings on the cross. He writes, p. 28: "Certain proper names in the Cynewulfian poems, particularly the *Elene*, seem to betray the influence of Irish-Latin orthography. Then when we examine the text of *Elene* itself, we discover many significant resemblances—some of them unique —to an Irish vernacular version [*Leabhar Breac*], whose Latin original . . . may be supposed to have been written in Ireland." However, see Claes Schaar, *Critical Studies in the Cynewulf Group* (Lund, 1949), p. 26.

40  *Pilgrimage of Arculfus*, ed. Macpherson, p. 10.

41  *Ibid.*, pp. 11–12.

42  *Ibid.*, p. 16.

43  See n. 32, above.

44  *Pilgrimage of Arculfus*, ed. Macpherson, p. 55.

45  *Ibid.*, p. 56.

46  Carleton F. Brown, "The Autobiographical Element in the Cynewulfian Rune Passages," *Englische Studien*, XXXVIII (1907), 196–233; also his "Cynewulf and Alcuin," *PMLA*, XVIII (1903), 308–34.

47  See Chapter III, n. 65, above.

48 See *Exeter Book,* eds. Krapp and Dobbie, pp. 33–35, ll. 1081–176 of *Christ.* The presence at Lindisfarne of a possibly Irish-transmitted contribution to Cynewulf's artistic scheme in the *Christ* is suggested by Kenneth Mildenberger, "Unity of Cynewulf's *Christ* in the Light of Iconography," *Speculum,* XXIII (1948), 426–32. The object of his study is St. Cuthbert's coffin, "fashioned in Northumbria, the home of Cynewulf," "built only a few years before the eighth century, to which period the composition of *Christ* is ascribed," and whose "incised figures exhibit most of the conventional elements of the Oriental Ascension iconography ingeniously adapted to the box-shape" (p. 431). On perpetual display at Lindisfarne, the Coptic elements on the coffin's sides may be compared with those in other Celtic and Anglo-Saxon examples, perhaps imported to Northumbria from the eastern Mediterranean through Ireland and Iona in the seventh or eighth centuries.

CHAPTER VII

1 See the facsimile of fol. 19b in the New Palaeographical Society's *Facsimiles of Ancient Manuscripts,* eds. Sir Edward M. Thompson and others (London, 1903–12), first series, I, Pl. 9; also see almost any folio of the complete photographic facsimile edition, *Exeter Book,* with intro. by Chambers, Förster, and Flower.

2 For examples of ruling, see the *Exeter Book,* with intro. by Chambers, Förster, and Flower, fols. 23b, 29b, 33b.

3 *Ibid.,* fol. 98a, ":-finit:-." The usual Irish signature for a Gospel text was *finit,* whereas Continental scribes preferred *explicit.* See *Palaeographia Latina,* ed. W. M. Lindsay (London, 1923), Pt. II, 5–9.

4 See the recent highly speculative theory argued by James Carney, *Studies in Irish Literature and History* (Dublin, 1955), pp. 77–128. It is suggested that the *Beowulf* poet used a "text known in Irish schools and based in part on Isidore of Seville" in constructing the genealogy of Grendel. Carney also believes that the *Beowulf* poet adapted an incident from the *Táin Bó Fraích* that had originally appeared in Adamnan's *Vita Columbae.* He writes, pp. 86–87: "*Beowulf* and *TBF* might well have been written by two friends, the one an Irishman the other a Saxon, both students of Adomnán and acquainted with each other's literary activity." Previously John R. Tolkien, "Beowulf: The Monsters and the Critics," *Proceedings of the British Academy,* XXII (1936), 245–95, suggested that an "inquisitive and less severe Celtic learning" might account for sympathetic treat-

ment of the illustrious pre-Christian past in the poem. Charles Donahue, "Beowulf, Ireland and the Natural Good," *Traditio,* VII (1949–51), 263–77, writes: "The good, but non-Christian ancestors whom the *Beowulf*-poet placed in the third city between darkness and the light of revelation" are contemporary with an Irish "third city . . . peopled with figures who are comparable, particularly in their moral and theological orientation to Beowulf and, even more, to Hrothgar." In "Grendel and the *Clanna Cain,*" *Journal of Celtic Studies,* I (1950), 167–75, Donahue shows that a passage from the Irish *Sex Aetates Mundi* is the "closest known relative of the *Beowulf*-passage" (ll. 111–14). See also Margaret W. Pepperdene, "Irish Christianity and *Beowulf,*" (Unpublished Ph.D. dissertation, Vanderbilt University, 1953), summarized in *Dissertation Abstracts,* XIII, No. 5, 798–99.

5 Wilhelm S. Teuffel, *History of Roman Literature,* rev. and enl. by Ludwig Schwabe; trans. G. C. Warr (London, 1891), I, 111.

6 Cicero, *De inventione,* trans. H. M. Hubbell (Cambridge, Mass., 1949), pp. 343–45.

7 Quintilian, *Institutio Oratoria,* trans. H. E. Butler (London, 1922), IV, 327. Quintilian's reference is to "funeral or consolatory speeches [in which] the delivery will be melancholy and subdued."

8 Tacitus, *The Works of Tacitus,* Oxford trans. rev. (London, 1901), II, 316–17.

9 *Glossarium mediae et infimae Latinitatis,* rev. ed. by Léopold Faure (Niort and London, 1885), V, 17.

10 *Reliques of Ancient English Poetry,* ed. Thomas Percy (London, 1883), I, xxv.

11 Thomas Warton, *History of English Poetry* (London, 1871), I, 5.

12 *Illustrations of Anglo-Saxon Poetry,* ed. W. Conybeare, p. 245.

13 *Ibid.,* p. 250.

14 Isaac Disraeli, *Amenities of Literature* (London, 1841), I, 55.

15 Ernst Sieper, *Die Altenglische Elegie* (Strassburg, 1915), p. 77. See also, G. Ehrismann, "Religiongeschichtliche Beiträge zum germanischen Frühchristentum," *Beiträge zur Geschichte der Deutschen Sprache und Literatur,* XXXV (1909), 230.

16 Pons, *Le Thème et le Sentiment de la Nature dans la Poésie Anglo-Saxonne,* p. 3.

17 *Ibid.,* p. 114.

18 *Ibid.,* p. 115. However, see Eugene F. Bradford, "Anglo-Saxon Melancholy," in *Harvard University Summaries of Theses,* 1927 (Cambridge, 1931), pp. 149–50, who concludes that "allegations of Celtic influence upon Anglo-Saxon melancholy" are unwarranted and that melancholy is "innate in the character of the

Anglo-Saxon people." See also *Old English Elegies,* trans. C. W. Kennedy (Princeton, 1936), p. 3.

19  See, however, George K. Anderson, *The Literature of the Anglo-Saxons* (Princeton, 1949). He sees the pagan element as "superior both as regards depth and as regards vividness" to the Christian. Behind the lyric, as behind the epic, lay "an aristocratic bardic tradition" (pp. 154–55). Of *Deor's Lament* he writes: " . . . a strictly lyric form before any Christian allusion comes in to mar the picture" (p. 155). Of the *Wanderer*: " . . . only the last few lines of the poem, which are weak and intrusive, seek the conventional road of Christian teaching . . ." (p. 159). The *Seafarer* "for all its pagan vitality, did not escape the almost inevitable Christian adulteration" (p. 161).

20  See also *Exodus,* 282–91; *Genesis,* 1371–435; *Guthlac,* 55, 1300–09; *Andreas,* 489–92, 369–76; the *Wanderer,* 46–48; *Riddles* III and IV. See Robert A. Kissack, *The Sea in Anglo-Saxon and Middle English Poetry* (St. Louis, 1926).

21  Olaf S. Anderson, *The Seafarer* (Lund, 1937), p. 16: "He is familiar with the cliffs, and knows the seabirds that nest on them (11. 20 ff.); he may have seen ships from afar sailing close to a rocky shore, and he can guess what hardships their crews may be exposed to. . . . The whole attitude of the poet shows that he has no actual sea-voyage in mind."

22  Dorothy Whitelock, "The Interpretation of the *Seafarer,*" in *The Early Cultures of North-West Europe,* eds. Cyril Fox and Bruce Dickins (Cambridge, 1950), p. 271. See also Stanley B. Greenfield, "The Theme of Spiritual Exile in *Christ I,*" *Philological Quarterly,* XXXII (1953), 321–28.

23  See I. L. Gordon, "Traditional Themes in *The Wanderer* and *The Seafarer,*" *Review of English Studies,* New Series, V (1954), pp. 2, 3, and 10. If the elegiac poet needed a model for a discourse on the lonely life of the self-exiled cleric he had but to observe closely the change of seasons along the North Sea coast north of the Wash. Indeed, a winter spent at a coastal monastery like Lindisfarne was probably not too unlike a wintertime voyage by curragh. Whereas Aidan and his band endured torrential and continuous rain as they made their way from Iona, their successors at Lindisfarne had to become acclimated to wind that might blow "a moderate to strong gale on one day in six throughout the year."—Richard Perry, *A Naturalist on Lindisfarne* (London, 1946), p. 70. Drawn to Lindisfarne by the lure of over two hundred species of birds, Perry complains of the driving sand and piercing cold "against which no combination of warm clothing is proof." He describes twelve-foot

snow drifts left by fifty mile an hour blizzards and tells of one
three-week stretch when the wind blew a continuous gale chiefly
out of the north (pp. 84, 186). On one occasion "spring-tide
walls of spray dashed over the fifty-foot cliffs . . . and right
over the hundred-foot battlements of the Castle into a field
two hundred yards from the Crag." Cf. the first ten lines of
the *Seafarer*. Perry reports watching gulls "swinging freely and
fearlessly on the storming seawinds for miles along the upper
edge of dune and cliff in a perpetual planing, head to wind,
to and fro across the onshore gales: now up-coast, now down
. . . " (p. 187). He observed kittiwakes, gannets, and petrels,
also, and his systematic lists include the white-tailed eagle, the
whooper swan, the herring gull, the arctic tern, and the cuckoo,
all birds probably observed by the *Seafarer* poet (ll. 18–25).
See Margaret E. Goldsmith, "The *Seafarer* and the Birds," *Review of English Studies,* New Series, V (1954), p. 235: " . . .
it is reasonable to argue that the writer of this passage had
first-hand knowledge of the sea-birds which frequent these
coasts, and had a particular interest in them."

24 *Exeter Book,* eds. Krapp and Dobbie, pp. 227–29.

25 Gildas, *Works,* in *Six Old Eng. Chron.,* ed. Giles, pp. 295, 311–12.
*Alcvini . . . Epistolae, MGH, Epist.,* IV, 56–57.

26 *Councils and Ecclesiastical Documents,* eds. Haddan and Stubbs,
I, 7–9.

27 Robin G. Collingwood, *The Archaeology of Roman Britain* (Lon-
don, 1930), pp. 113–51. See also Francis J. Haverfield, "Early
Northumbrian Christianity and the Altars to the 'Di Veteres,' "
*Archeologia Aeliana,* XV, 3rd Series (1918), 22-43.

28 *H. E.,* III, 16. See also Browne, *British Latin Selections,* pp. 4–5.

29 A similar account of the Bangor calamity is given by Geoffrey
of Monmouth (*Historia Regum Britanniae,* XI, 12–13) with one
change. Geoffrey's version has the Bangor monks killed for refusing subjugation to Augustine. See *The Legendary History of
Britain: Geoffrey of Monmouth's Historia Regum Britanniae,* ed.
John S. P. Tatlock (Berkeley and Los Angeles, 1950), p. 65.

30 *The Anglo-Saxon Chronicle,* ed. and trans. Benjamin Thorpe, Rolls
Series (London, 1861), II, 18–19.

31 *The Annals of Clonmacnoise,* ed. Murphy, p. 99.

32 *The Annals of Inisfallen,* ed. and trans. Sean MacAirt (Dublin,
1951), pp. 84–85.

33 *Annals of Ulster,* ed. Hennessy, I, 87.

34 *Annales Cambriae,* ed. John Williams, Rolls Series (London,
1860), p. 6. See also, Nora K. Chadwick, "Early Culture and

Learning in North Wales," in *Studies in the Early British Church,* ed. Chadwick (Cambridge, 1958), p. 68.

35  Thomas O'Rahilly, *Early Irish History and Mythology* (Dublin, 1946), pp. 253–55, 506–7.

36  W. F. Skene, *The Four Ancient Books of Wales* (Edinburgh, 1868), I, 233–35.

37  William of Malmesbury, *De gest. pont.,* p. 326.

38  *The Itinerary in Wales of John Leland in or about the Years 1536–1539,* ed. Lucy Toulmin Smith (London, 1906), Pt. VI, p. 68.

39  Thomas Pennant, *Tours in Wales,* ed. John Rhys (Caernarvon, 1883), I, 285; Rice Rees, *An Essay on the Welsh Saints* (London, 1836), p. 182.

40  Gildas, *Works,* in *Six Old Eng. Chron.,* ed. Giles, p. 299, lists twenty-eight Romano-British cities that were destroyed. The lines in the *Wanderer* (74–76) and other references to crumbling walls in the Old English corpus attest to the impact which ruined forts and camps had on the poet.

41  Heinrich Leo, *Carmen anglosaxonicum in codice Exoniensi quod vulgo inscribitur Ruinae* (Halle, 1865), p. 5. Also John Earle, "An Ancient Saxon Poem of a City in Ruins Supposed to be Bath," *Proceedings of the Bath Natural History and Antiquarian Field Club,* II (1872), 259–70; more recently Cecilia A. Hotchner, *Wessex and Old English Poetry* (New York, 1939). See Stephen J. Herben, "The Ruin," *Modern Language Notes,* LIV (1939), 37–39. He suggests the Roman Wall as the site described in the poem. See also *Modern Language Notes,* LIX (1944), 72–74.

42  *Select Translations,* eds. Cook and Tinker, p. 57.

43  *Ibid.,* p. 56.

44  Joseph Hemingway, *History of the City of Chester* (Chester, 1831), I, Pt. I, 20–21; also Robert E. Wheeler, *Prehistoric and Roman Wales* (Oxford, 1925), p. 222.

45  *The Historical Works of Giraldus Cambrensis,* ed. Thomas Wright (London, 1887), p. 372.

46  Neaverson, *Mediaeval Castles,* p. 1. F. J. Haverfield, *Catalogue of the Roman Inscribed and Sculptured Stones in the Grosvenor Museum* (Chester, 1900), p. 14. Red sandstone walls and pillars were uncovered at Chester in 1863. See Thomas Hughes, *The Stranger's Handbook to Chester* (Chester, n. d.), p. 86.

47  Neaverson, *Mediaeval Castles,* pp. 3–4.

48  Higden, *Polychronicon,* II, 79.

49  *Ibid.*

50  F. J. Haverfield, "Romano-British Somerset," in *The Victoria His-*

*tory of the County of Somerset,* ed. William Page (London, 1906), I, 224.

51 It is likely that the *Ruin* poet had been exposed to *De locis sanctis,* the narrative of a Gaulish bishop's journey through the Holy Land transcribed at Iona by Adamnan and widely read in Northumbria (see Chap. III, n. 65, above). Adamnan gives Arculf's account of Hebron: " . . . once the metropolis of the Philistines and inhabited by giants . . . traces of the city, which was long ago destroyed, appear in remnants of ruins . . . remains of the destroyed walls [are] scattered over the surface of the plain. . . ." Adamnan also gives Arculf's impression of the destroyed city of Jericho.—*Pilgrimage of Arculfus,* trans. Macpherson, pp. 31–32, 35. The parallel between the fate of the Holy Land cities and the desolate, devastated centers of former Roman strength such as Chester might well have suggested itself to the elegiac poet.

52 Lea, *History of Sacerdotal Celibacy,* I, 123–124.

53 *Ibid.*

54 *Sacrorum conciliorum nova, et amplissima collectio,* ed. Giovanni Mansi (Paris, 1901), II, col. 679: "Interdixit per omnia magna synodus, non episcopo, non presbytero, non diacono, nec alicui omnino qui in clero est, licere subintroductam habere mulierem: nisi forte aut matrem, aut sororem, aut amitam, vel eas tantum personas, quae suspicionem effugiunt."

55 *Subintroductae* are defined as "Mulieres quarum commercium et habitationem vitare jubentur clerici; femmes suspectes dont la cohabitation était interdite aux ecclésiastiques."—W. H. Maigne d'Arnis, *Lexicon: Manuale ad scriptores mediae et infimae Latinitatis* (Paris, 1866), col. 2124. For *focaria* and *focarista* see col. 943.

56 Dom Louis Gougaud, "Mulierum Consortia: Étude sur le syneisaktisme chez les ascètes celtiques," *Ériu,* IX (1921–23), 153. For James Carney's disagreement with Gougaud see "A Chrínóc, Cubaid Do Cheól," *Eigse,* IV (1943–44), 280–83. Also see Thomas Olden, "On the *Consortia* of the First Order of Irish Saints," *Proceedings of the Royal Irish Academy,* III (1893–96), 415–20.

57 See Browne, *British Latin Selections,* pp. 3–4. He writes: "It does not exhibit the weird vocabulary of the *H. F. [Hisperica Famina]*; but its puerile syntax is quite in the Hisperic manner. It breathes the spirit of Celtic monasticism." See also *Hisperica Famina,* ed. Jenkinson, p. 33.

58 Macalister, *Corpus inscriptionum insularum Celticarum,* I, 310. Jackson, *Lang. and Hist. in Early Britain,* p. 670, dates the Saturninus stone *circa* 525. Hodgkin, *History of the Anglo-Saxons,*

I, 249, believes that "many of these Celtic saints were, in fact, but well-born clerks in holy orders: men of sufficient wealth to be able to found and endow the small churches and monasteries which have perpetuated their names. Such a one was, for example, Saturninus, whose tombstone tells the world that by [his side] there was laid his 'holy consort'." See also Victor Nash-Williams, *The Early Christian Monuments of Wales* (Cardiff, 1950), p. 63, #33, for a sixth-century inscription at Llantrisant: " . . . a most holy woman, lies here, who was the very loving wife of Bivatig(irnus), servant of God, bishop (?priest), and disciple of Paulinus. . . ."

59 Paul Grosjean, "Édition et commentaire du *Catalogus Sanctorum Hiberniae secundum diversa tempora* ou *De Tribus Ordinibus Sanctorum Hiberniae,*" *Analecta Bollandiana,* LXXIII (1955), 197–213; 289–322. This is the first really usable and reliable edition of this document based on all extant texts. See particularly p. 206.

60 *Ibid.,* p. 206.

61 *Félire Óengusso Céli Dé,* ed. Stokes, p. 41.

62 William of Malmesbury, *De gest. pont.,* ed. Hamilton, p. 358.

63 See *Bede,* ed. A. Hamilton Thompson (Oxford, 1935), pp. 80–81. Whitby is an example of a community whose *familia* was made up of both monks and nuns presided over by an abbess. Similar arrangements existed at Coldingham and Hartlepool. After King Aldfrith's death in 705, "Under the pretense of founding religious communities worldly minded laymen had bought lands from the king for themselves and their heirs. . . . These institutions were . . . ruled by married men with families, whose wives were sometimes heads of *soi-disant* nunneries."

64 *Councils,* eds. Haddan and Stubbs, III, 195.

65 *Lives of Saints,* ed. Stokes, p. x. Fursa's mission is probably responsible for the Irish hanging bowls and clasps found in the Sutton Hoo treasure of an East Anglian king.—See Françoise Henry, "Irish Enamels of the Dark Ages and their Relation to the Cloisonné Techniques," *Dark-Age Britain,* ed. Harden, pp. 81–88.

66 Translated as *Liadain and Curithir* by Kuno Meyer (London, 1902). The stanzas here are from *Early Irish Lyrics,* ed. Murphy (Oxford, 1956), p. 85. James Carney, *Studies in Irish Literature and History,* p. 220, writes: "This story is confused and improbable but has suggestions of beauty about it that give us a better idea than any other story of what must have been the form of the primitive *Tristan.*" For an attempt to point out the classical ring in the poem see John J. Savage, "An Old Irish

Version of Laodamia and Protesilaus," in *Classical and Medieval Studies in Honor of Edward Kennard Rand* (New York, 1938), pp. 265–72.

67 *Early Irish Lyrics,* ed. Murphy, p. 209. The Northumbrians might well have known the story of Conall Corc (*circa* 400), banished to Scotland by his uncle who "wrote on his shield a request in oghams that he be put to death instantly." Friendly intervention causes the oghams to be changed and Conall is introduced to a chief's daughter who falls in love with him. Her life is endangered when her father finds that Conall is an exile. They stay in Scotland until she has produced three sons, afterward returning to Ireland where Conall reclaims his kingdom.— Nora K. Chadwick, "Pictish and Celtic Marriage in Early Literary Tradition," *Scottish Gaelic Studies,* VIII, Pt. 1 (1955), 56–115. Secular tales of this sort could easily have made their way to Northumbria after 635 via missionary routes. For a provocative article along this line, see Nora K. Chadwick's "The Lost Literature of Celtic Scotland," *Scottish Gaelic Studies,* VII, Pt. 2 (1953), 115–83. She discusses the tradition of a northern Arthur, possibly transmitted to South Wales from Strathclyde in the eighth century by refugee ecclesiastics of the British church.

68 *Early Irish Lyrics,* p. 85. Murphy writes (p. 209): "Líadan followed him to his monastic cell in the Déisi. Cuirithir sailed across the sea from her, and later Líadan died praying upon the stone upon which he used to pray in the Déisi. The poem . . . would seem to have been uttered by Líadan before Cuirithir sailed away."

69 *Select Translations,* ed. Cook and Tinker, p. 64.

70 *Ibid.,* p. 65.

71 *Selections from Ancient Irish Poetry,* trans. Kuno Meyer (London, 1928), pp 37–38. However, see James Carney, "The Impact of Christianity," in *Early Irish Society,* ed. Myles Dillon (Dublin, 1954), pp. 75–76. He sees the poem as an "elaborately worked out metaphor" done by a priest in his old age who finds a copy of the *Book of Psalms,* "the very copy which had been his first lesson book. He addresses it in metaphorical terms as a woman called Crínóc, or 'Dear little old thing,' whom he had first known and loved as a boy of seven."

72 Oscar D. Watkins, *A History of Penance* (London, 1920), II, 606–11; also Thomas P. Oakley, "Cultural Affiliations of Early Ireland in the Penitentials," *Speculum,* VIII (1933), 489–500; John T. McNeill, *A History of the Cure of Souls* (New York, 1951), 112–36. For evidence of the direct influence of Celtic concepts of sin on Old English homilies, see Morton Bloomfield,

*The Seven Deadly Sins* (East Lansing, 1952), pp. 115–17.

73 See John T. McNeill and Helena M. Gamer, *Medieval Handbooks of Penance* (New York, 1938), pp. 161, 166, 252.

74 Helen Waddell, *Mediaeval Latin Lyrics,* 5th ed. (London, 1948), pp. 68–69.

CHAPTER VIII

1 C. R. O'Cleirigh's review of *Studies in Early British History,* ed. Chadwick, in *Éigse,* VIII (1955), 81. All students of Insular culture will be indebted to Wilfrid Bonser's *An Anglo-Saxon and Celtic Bibliography* (Oxford, 1957), 2 vols. See Bertram Colgrave, *The Venerable Bede and His Times* (Jarrow-on-Tyne, 1958).

2 Charles W. Jones, *Saints' Lives and Chronicles in Early England* (Ithaca, 1947), pp. 177–78. See also R. M. Wilson, *The Lost Literature of Medieval England* (New York, 1952), p. 104.

3 See Chapter VII, n. 1, above; also *The Vercelli Book,* ed. Krapp, p. xxxvii, where the possibility of an Irish source for the Old English *Fates of the Apostles* is raised.

4 See Bishop, *Liturgica Historica,* pp. 251–55. He suggests that the English Feast of the Conception has its origin in Irish metrical calendars like the *Martyrology of Oengus.* In one tenth-century English calendar, he notes twenty-four Irish entries out of a total of 365.

5 See Charles J. Singer, "Early English Magic and Medicine," *Proceedings of the British Academy,* IX (1920), 360–62. The utilization of the so-called "circle of Columba" legend in an Old English manuscript of the eleventh century (MS Cot. Vit. E xviii, fol. 13v) is pointed out. In Ireland, the "circle of Columba" is identified by archaeologists as a "large flat stone into the surface of which there has been cut in remote antiquity a design consisting of a cross surrounded by a circle." Magical powers were ascribed to such stones and their use passed over to Brittain. The figure of a circle with a cross inscribed within it appears in the Old English manuscript accompanied by the legend "þis is sancte Columcille circul," in addition to a charm for bees. In an Old English book of devotions, dating from the fifteenth century, Columba is invoked in an incantation designed to extinguish the flames of a burning house.

# Bibliography

The following references are mainly those cited frequently in the notes. In the chapter notes, all citations of items in this list occur in abbreviated form. Other sources not listed here are given in full at first citation in each chapter.

Adamnan. *Adamnani Vita S. Columbae,* ed. J. T. Fowler. New ed. rev. Oxford, 1920.

——. *De locis sanctis.* Translated under the title *The Pilgrimage of Arculfus in the Holy Land* by J. R. Macpherson. Palestine Pilgrims' Text Society, Vol. III, No. 1, 1895.

——. *The Life of St. Columba,* ed. William Reeves. With an English translation prepared under the superintendence of the Bishop of Brechin, and the notes rearranged by W. F. Skene. *Historians of Scotland,* Vol. VI. Edinburgh, 1874.

*Aedilvulfi Carmen. See* Ethelwulf.

Alcuin. *Alcvini sive Albini Epistolae,* in *Epistolae Karolini Aevi,* II, ed. Ernst Dümmler. *Monum. Germ. Hist., Epistolarum,* IV. Berlin, 1895.

*Anglo-Saxon Minor Poems,* ed. Elliott V. K. Dobbie. New York, 1942.

*The Annals of Clonmacnoise,* ed. and trans. Denis Murphy. Dublin, 1896.

*Annals of Ulster,* Vol. I, ed. and trans. W. M. Hennessy. Dublin, 1887.

*The Antiphonary of Bangor,* ed. F. E. Warren. Facsimile and letter-press edition. London, 1893.

Bede, The Venerable. *Baedae Opera historica.* With an English translation by J. E. King. London, 1930. 2 vols.

——. *Venerabilis Baedae Historiam ecclesiasticam gentis Anglorum . . . commentario tam critico quam historico instruxit Carolus Plummer.* Oxford, 1896. 2 vols.

Bishop, Edmund. *Liturgica Historica.* Oxford, 1918.

Bowen, Emrys G. *The Settlements of the Celtic Saints in Wales.* Cardiff, 1954.

Brown, G. Baldwin. *The Arts in Early England,* Vols. V and VI. London, 1930 and 1937.

Browne, R. A. *British Latin Selections.* Oxford, 1954.

Brüning, Getrud. "Adamnans Vita Columbae und ihre Ableitungen," *Zeitschrift für Celtische Philologie,* XI (1917).

*Carmina Gadelica,* ed. Alexander Carmichael. Edinburgh, 1900.

*Codices Latini Antiquiores,* ed. E. A. Lowe, Vols. II and VII. Oxford, 1935 and 1956.

Cook, Albert S. "The Possible Begetter of the Old English *Beowulf* and *Widsith*," *Transactions of the Connecticut Society of Arts and Sciences,* XXV (1922).

*Councils and Ecclesiastical Documents Relating to Great Britain and Ireland,* eds. Arthur West Haddan and William Stubbs. Oxford, 1869–71.

*Dark-Age Britain,* ed. Donald B. Harden. London, 1956.

Dugdale, Sir William. *Monasticon Anglicanum.* London, 1846.

*Early Irish Lyrics,* ed. and trans. Gerard Murphy. Oxford, 1956.

*Early Sources of Scottish History,* ed. and trans. Alan O. Anderson. Edinburgh, 1922. Vol. I.

Ethelwulf. *Aedilvulfi Carmen,* in *Poetae Latini Aevi Carolini,* I, ed. Ernst Dümmler. *Monum. Germ. Hist., Poetarum Latinorum Medii Aevi,* I. Berlin, 1881, 582–604.

*Evangeliorum Quattuor: Codex Cenannensis.* Complete facsimile edition of the Book of Kells, including 48 plates in full color and 652 plates in monochrome. Edition limited to 500 copies on handmade paper. Introduction by the late E. H. Alton; study of illuminations by Peter Meyer; full collation of the text with the Vulgate by G. O. Simms. Berne, 1950–51. 3 vols.

*Evangeliorum Quattuor: Codex Lindisfarnensis.* Complete facsimile edition of the Lindisfarne Gospels, including 28 plates in full color and 480 in monochrome. Edition limited to 650 copies. Paleographic introduction by T. J. Brown; study of the art and ornament by R. Bruce-Mitford; commentary on the Anglo-Saxon glosses by A. S. C. Ross. Olten and Lausanne, 1956–59. 2 vols. (Vol. II with commentary, etc., was not available to the author when this study was made.)

*The Exeter Book of Old English Poetry.* With introductory chapters by R. W. Chambers, Max Förster, and Robin Flower. London, 1933.

*The Exeter Book,* eds. George P. Krapp and Elliott V. K. Dobbie. New York, 1936.

*The Exeter Book,* Part II, ed. and trans. W. S. Mackie. London, 1934.

*Félire Óengusso Céli Dé,* ed. and trans. Whitley Stokes. London, 1905.

Förster, Max. *Keltisches Wortgut im Englischen.* Halle, 1921.

Fox, Sir Cyril. *The Personality of Britain.* Cardiff, 1943.

Gildas. *The Works of Gildas,* in *Six Old English Chronicles,* ed. and trans. J. A. Giles. London, 1848.

Gougaud, Louis. *Christianity in Celtic Lands.* London, 1932.

Henry, Françoise. *Irish Art in the Early Christian Period.* London, 1940.

Herbert, John A. *Illuminated Manuscripts.* London, 1911.

Higden, Ranulf. *Polychronicon Ranulphi Higden Monachi Cestrensis,* ed. Churchill Babington. Rolls Series. London, 1869. Vol. II.

*The Hisperica Famina,* ed. Francis H. Jenkinson. Cambridge, 1908.

*History of the Church of Ireland,* ed. Walter A. Phillips. Oxford, 1933, Vol. I.

Hodgkin, R. H. *A History of the Anglo-Saxons,* 3rd ed. London, 1952. Vol. I.

*Illustrations of Anglo-Saxon Poetry,* ed. William Conybeare. London, 1826.

Jackson, K. H. *Language and History in Early Britain.* Edinburgh, 1953.

Kenney, James F. *The Sources for the Early History of Ireland.* New York, 1929. Vol. I.

Knight, G. A. Frank. *Archaeological Light on the Early Christianizing of Scotland.* London, 1933. 2 vols.

Laistner, M. L. W. *Thought and Letters in Western Europe.* 2nd ed. Ithaca, 1957.

Lawlor, Henry C. *The Monastery of St. Mochaoi of Nendrum.* Belfast, 1925.

Lawlor, Hugh J. "The Cathach of St. Columba," *Proceedings of the Royal Irish Academy,* XXXIII (1916).

Lea, Henry C. *History of Sacerdotal Celibacy in the Christian Church.* 3rd ed. London, 1907. Vol. I.

Lindsay, W. M. *Early Irish Minuscule Script.* Oxford, 1910.

*Lives of Saints from the Book of Lismore,* ed. and trans. Whitley Stokes. Oxford, 1890.

Luce, A. A. "The *Book of Kells* and the *Gospels of Lindisfarne—*

A Comparison," *Hermathena*, LXXIX (May, 1952) and LXXX (Nov., 1952).

Macalister, R. A. S. *The Archaeology of Ireland.* London, 1928.

——. *Corpus inscriptionum insularum Celticarum.* Dublin, 1945. Vol. I.

Mackinlay, James M. *Ancient Church Dedications in Scotland.* Edinburgh, 1915. 2 vols.

Masai, François. *Essai sur les origines de la miniature dite Irlandaise.* Brussels, 1947.

Morey, Charles R. *Mediaeval Art.* New York, 1942.

Neaverson, Ernest. *Mediaeval Castles in North Wales.* London, 1947.

O'Curry, Eugene. *Lectures on the Manuscript Materials of Ancient Irish History.* Dublin, 1861.

*Pilgrimage of Arculfus in the Holy Land. See* Adamnan, *De locis sanctis.*

Pons, Émile. *Le Thème et le Sentiment de la Nature dans la Poésie Anglo-Saxonne.* Strasbourg, 1925.

Porter, Arthur K. *The Crosses and Culture of Ireland.* New Haven, 1931.

Raine, James. *The History and Antiquities of North Durham.* London, 1852.

Roger, Maurice. *L'Enseignment des lettres classiques d'Ausone à Alcuin.* Paris, 1905.

Ryan, John. *Irish Monasticism.* Dublin, 1931.

*The Sculptured Stones of Scotland,* ed. John Stuart. Aberdeen, 1867. Vol. II.

*Select Translations from Old English Poetry,* eds. Albert S. Cook and Chauncey B. Tinker. Cambridge, Mass., 1935.

Schiaparelli, Luigi. "Note paleografiche intorno all' origine e ad alcuni caratteri della scrittura e del sistema abbreviativo irlandese," *Archivio storico Italiano,* LXXIV (1916), Pt. II, 3 *et seq.*

Skene, W. F. *Celtic Scotland.* Edinburgh, 1887. Vol. II.

Slover, Clark H. "Early Literary Channels between Britain and Ireland," in Univ. of Texas *Studies in English,* No. 6 and No. 7. Austin, 1926 and 1927.

Stevens, William O. *The Cross in the Life and Literature of the Anglo-Saxons.* New York, 1904.

*Studies in Early British History,* ed. Nora K. Chadwick. Cambridge, 1954.

*Studies in the Early British Church,* ed. Nora K. Chadwick. Cambridge, 1958.

Symeon of Durham. *Symeonis Monachi Opera omnia,* Vol. I, *His-*

*toria Ecclesiae Dunhelmensis,* ed. Thomas Arnold. Rolls Series. London, 1882.

*Thesaurus Palaeohibernicus,* eds. Whitley Stokes and John Strachan. Cambridge, 1903. 2 vols.

Thompson, Sir Edward M. *Handbook of Greek and Latin Paleography.* International Scientific Series, Vol. LXX. New York, 1893.

*The Vercelli Book,* ed. George P. Krapp. New York, 1932.

*Vitae Sanctorum Hiberniae,* ed. Charles Plummer. Oxford, 1910. 2 vols.

Wattenbach, Wilhelm. *Das Schriftwesen im Mittelalter.* Leipzig, 1875.

William of Malmesbury. *Willelmi Malmesbiriensis monachi De gestis pontificum Anglorum,* ed. N. E. S. Hamilton. Rolls Series. London, 1870.

# Index

Abbots, Irish: method for choosing successor of, 30

Abingdon: Irish elements in the founding tradition of, 25, 109–10 n44

Adamnan (ninth abbot of Iona): friendly relations with King Aldfrith, 28, 91; author of *Vita S. Columbae,* 37, of *De locis sanctis,* 37, of possible scholia on *Eclogues* and *Georgics* of Virgil, 37; *De locis sanctis* dedicated to King Aldfrith, 39; visits Bamburgh and King Aldfrith, 116 n54. *See also De locis sanctis;* Schaffhausen Adamnan; *Vita S. Columbae*

*Aedilvulfi Carmen:* composed by Ethelwulf, 25; references to Irish scribe and blacksmith in, 26

Aileran (monk of Clonard): his *Interpretatio mystica progenitorum,* 36–37

Alcuin: his estimate of King Aldfrith, 28; writes to *Familia* at Lindisfarne after Norse raid, 83, 87

Aldfrith (king of Northumbria): visits Melrose, 25; rules Northumbria, 27; references to, in Irish annals, 28; references to, by Bede, 28; Alcuin's estimate of, 28; Irish verses attributed to, 29; Irish name for, 29; Aldhelm, a friend of, 89; patron of Insular learning, 91; stay at Iona as prince-in-exile, 94; traditions concerning, 112 n4; letters to, from Aldhelm, 114 n39

Aldhelm: friend of King Aldfrith, 89

Antiphonary of Bangor: contents of, 40, 117 n1; published by Muratori in 1770, 41; characteristics of scribal hand in, 47, 49; features of its preparation, 49; mentioned, 94

Arnold, Matthew: his "St. Brandan," 4

Bamburgh: location in relation to Lindisfarne, 15; seat of Northumbrian kings, 94; mentioned, 83

Bangor (Ireland): monastery at, 121 n44